TWISTED HUMOUR

Mary Wood

MINERVA PRESS

LONDON

ATLANTA MONTREUX SYDNEY

First Published 1998 by
MINERVA PRESS
195 Knightsbridge
London SW7 1RE

Printed in Great Britain for Minerva Press

TWISTED HUMOUR

For Harvey, Matthew, Richard and Maxine
with love

Ideas have been flowing from those I know
for about a couple of years or so,
I'm grateful to all for their support
Too many to name, I've to keep this short!

I thank my pals at Seven Seas
For helping me with some of these
My beloved family have assisted too
Their support is valued and ever true!

I dedicate this book to those above
The ones for whom I care and love
To my readers, too, across the miles
I wish you all long-distance smiles!

About the Author

Mary was born on 31st July, 1954, the eldest of seven children, and enjoyed a happy childhood on the family farm near Coventry in Warwickshire. She still lives in a farming environment in Preston, East Yorkshire, where she has settled with her husband and their three children. She works as a senior secretary for a well-known healthcare company and, when she is not at work or writing poetry, her time is occupied with family and home activities. Other interests include reading, swimming, dining out and visits to the theatre.

Mary's fascination for poetry began as a girl of eleven when her beloved parents gave her a still much-cherished poetry book. She has been writing private poems for family and friends for many years, but has only recently considered writing for a wider audience.

Mary believes her style of poetry will appeal to anyone with a sense of humour, in all walks of life. She has had countless hours of pleasure putting this collection together, drawn from reading, listening, observation, true life experiences and pure imagination, and says if the same degree of pleasure is derived by her readers, she has wholeheartedly achieved her goal.

Contents

The Morning after the Night Before

It was the morning after the night before
My eyes were heavy, my throat was sore,
The tears had subsided – there were no more to shed
As I lay downhearted alone in my bed.

Through misty glazed eyes the romantic in me
Had only seen what I wanted to see,
His bright blue eyes and sun-kissed hair,
His striking features – so debonair!

It was love at first sight, of that I was sure,
As our eyes met across the crowded floor.
His approach was swift – he asked me to dance,
The spell was cast – I was in a trance!

I was sure we had both fallen in love,
That, for each other, we were made in heaven above.
When later I left him for the powder room
I truly thought his face registered gloom!

But I returned to see him with a pretty girl
He held her close, re-arranged a curl.
Leaning forward, her cheek he tenderly kissed
She was so beautiful – how could he resist?

I turned and fled without a backward glance,
Disenchanted with this new romance
Tears were streaming down my wretched face,
How could he hold another in warm embrace?

Now the telephone rouses me from my desolation
It's him! My heart pounds, I feel wild elation
'Sorry,' he says, 'my feelings are true,
I care for my sister, but I'm in love with you!'

The Gruesome Delivery

It was a human hand, in a cardboard box
Delivered to Mrs Arnold Fox.
They'd carried out their threat for sure
Here was the proof at her own front door!

This meant her husband must be dead,
Would she next receive his head,
An ear, a toe, a foot or more
When next the postman tapped the door?

They had threatened to undertake this gruesome deed
With frightening menace, to satisfy greed,
If he did not settle his current debts
From senseless gambling and futile bets.

She thought he'd paid, he said he had,
She knew he was foolish, but not all bad
Just misguided in the judgements he made.
For this failing, with his life, he'd paid!

She hadn't seen him for several days
His work 'kept him away', to coin a phrase.
She'd expected him home later that night
But not in a parcel – it just wasn't right!

Blow Me!

The tot in the super-store was looking intently at me,
My trolley was laden as high as could be.
I approached the exit, he continued to stare
As he sat near the door in his little pushchair.

I stepped on the mat to operate the automatic doors
Devilishly puffed my cheeks and blew with force.
As the doors swung open, I peered the tot's way,
His stunned look of amazement made my day!

Hung Up!

The neighbour to the man, appeared all forlorn
As he called at his door, in the early morn
'Your wife,' said he, 'has hung herself on the washing line.'
Though the neighbour was distraught, the man seemed
    fine!

'I'm just off to work,' said the man, in haste,
'I'm afraid I don't have a minute to waste.
Can I ask a favour? If it looks like rain
Perhaps you'd kindly get her in again!'

Identical Twins

Identical twins were my sister and I,
People would stare, as we passed by.
Dressed alike, with no clues to impart
They never could tell us two apart!

What trouble and havoc we could wreak
When fun and mischief we would seek,
We'd confuse our friends and smile with glee
When which twin was which they couldn't see!

To tell us apart they suggested we wear
Different coloured ribbons in our hair,
This was fine if we both complied
But sometimes we didn't although we tried!

Then something happened to change this trend
On my nose, grew a boil, at the very end!
My sister escaped, a boil she had not
Her nose was clear, not even a spot!

Now it was easy to tell my twin from me,
The turn of our friends to smile with glee
For my red nose signified that I was me
So the other twin, they knew, was she!

Laced Up!

The rollerblader's lace had come untied.
As he stopped to fix it on the roadside
The rear bumper was an opportune support
On a delivery van, but his rollers got caught.

So there he was, his foot caught tight
As the van drew away, a comical sight,
Skating, one-legged, at speed so high
The van driver saw him; unaware of his tie!

For miles they travelled, as the van driver gazed
In his rear view mirror, he was truly amazed
At the rollerblader's tremendous staying power
Still right behind, at ninety miles an hour!

When he stopped at last, he could plainly see
The rollerblader needed setting free,
But concerned for the wear on the road-used boot
He made him swap for the homeward route!

Very Bad Luck!

His nickname, at school, was 'Donald Duck',
Being called Donald was very bad luck
He didn't like being known by that name
But had to get used to it, all the same.

When he left the area, he was glad to be rid
Of the nickname that had haunted him as a kid.
At his new school, the nickname he never heard,
The 'Duck', after Donald, was a bygone word!

Until, on the sports field, he heard, 'Donald Duck!'
Disappointed, he turned round, to take a look
Who had discovered his secret, with dread
Just then, the ball struck him, hard, on the head!

The Bank Robber

The bank robber was naked, he wore nothing at all
Stunned were the staff – he had some gall
As he held them up, and money demanded
Not hesitating when, to him, it was handed.

He grabbed it and ran out of the door
As staff and customers rose from the floor
From positions he'd ordered when he appeared,
A naked bank robber, how very weird!

When the police arrived, their questions to ask
To establish his description proved an impossible task.
For though his face was uncovered and bare
Nobody's eyes had focused up there!

A Close Shave

The razor was sharp, as Sandy shaved himself
Replacing the can on the bathroom shelf
His steaming hot bath a welcome sight
For him to sink into – a cleansing delight!

He tugged off his trousers, socks and shirt,
Stood in his underpants, covered in dirt
Intending to remove them before stepping in,
Suddenly he was startled by an almighty din!

The aerosol had fallen, exploding on impact
In the steaming hot water, the mirrors all cracked.
Around him fell debris, the ceiling, a door
As he cowered, in a heap, on the bathroom floor.

Sandy stood where the bathroom had been
Even dirtier now, would he ever get clean?
Miraculously unhurt; saved from an early grave
Twice in minutes, he'd had a close shave!

Wiped Out

A telephone number was scrawled in the dirt,
Alan aimed the hose, the water to squirt
Over the car, to wipe it all out
His brother would be cross, without a doubt.

Over David's car, Alan drew the hose
Wiped out the digits, from start to close.
'It must be the number of his latest fling,'
Mused Alan, what upset his action would bring!

This was Alan's revenge on David, you see
For he'd teased him rotten and chuckled, with glee
When Alan had been feeling particularly low
After losing a girl he'd been keen to know.

Alan was satisfied he'd done his job well
Though, likely, David would make his life hell.
To meddle, in this way, he would view as cheek
When next they met, David was first to speak!

'Remember that girl you fell for last week
Whose number you've desperately tried to seek?
I saw her again, she feels the same for you
On my car, is her number, please ring her, do.'

David, still unaware of Alan's previous action,
Was surprised at his brother's adverse reaction.
He thought he was imparting some welcome news
But Alan was wiped out, with a fit of the blues!

The Siege

'Go away, you can't come in!'
Came a voice, from the house within,
'I'm holding a hostage, so stay away
If you want her alive, keep your men at bay!'

The officers moved back and stood well clear
Fearing for the lady whose residence was here.
The neighbours had alerted there was trouble afoot
The house under siege by this dangerous nut!

No one knew what reasons he had
To take this action, he must be mad.
His identity too was also unclear
The lady now, for her life, must fear!

They attempted to build a rapport with him
And tried the phone, but he just let it ring
It seemed their progress was going to be slow
They hoped they could persuade him to let her go.

Then, to the surprise of all those present
The lady in question walked into the crescent,
She'd been out shopping, unaware of the fuss,
'A man?' she said, 'it must be Russ!'

The officers were puzzled, she showed no alarm
In fact, she was amused and very calm.
'There is no mad man,' she laughed with glee,
'Russ is my parrot, he speaks, you see!'

The Fortune Teller

The young man was happy, even carefree
As he stepped into the caravan of Gypsy Roselee.
He'd never had his fortune told before
He was curious to know what lay in store.

She read his palm, used Tarot cards too,
Everything she said, he knew was true.
He sat in amazement, as she related his past
How did she know that? He was truly aghast!

Then the Gypsy fell silent deep in thought,
To the table, pen and paper, she brought.
She wrote some words, to see them he strived
She said not to read them until home he arrived.

Then abruptly she ended their interview,
He pocketed the note, from the van he withdrew
Though tempted to peek at the note, he resisted,
He must read it at home, she had firmly insisted!

He started his car, and headed for home
But lacked concentration, his mind started to roam
His driving was erratic, his speed increased
Just one more bend, then he was deceased!

To his young widow, the policeman had to say
'I'm sorry, your husband died in a crash today,
This was in his pocket, though I don't understand.'
'You have no future,' said the note in his hand!

The Bell Ringer

There was a bell ringer called Bower
Who rang the bell in the tower
In the rope she got caught
Against gravity she fought
As she shot like a bolt up the tower!

The Big Ass

There lived an ass who was a big ass
An ass, alas, nothing could pass
It would block the road
As along it strode
It was an ass of an ass to pass!

Charlie's Win

The pub competition was an annual event,
Charlie was persuaded when in he went
To guess the number of twenty pence bits
In the big glass jar – a game of wits!

He paid a pound for charity, to guess,
If right he'd win the jar no less.
With all the coins collected therein
He submitted his entry, with a grin.

One week later when he was comfortably installed
In the pub, the winner's name was called.
It was Charlie who'd won the competition outright,
So thrilled he was, with drink he got tight!

As he left the pub, the jar he carried
He tottered, swayed, lingered and tarried
With hundreds of coins, an appalling sight,
He got as far as his doorstep that night!

Then the jar he dropped, with a resounding crash
Out spilled all the shiny cash.
Too drunk to worry, he left it there
Entered the house without a care!

When morning came, he remembered the cash,
To recover his winnings, he made a dash.
Went to the doorstep, in disbelief to stare
Hundreds of milk bottles were lined up there!

The Masked Ball

He attended the Masked Ball, on his own, alone
As his wife was unwell, with migraine, so prone,
But she later recovered and decided to go
Donning her costume, but was in for a blow!

Her husband was having the time of his life
Unaware he was watched by his angry wife,
Her costume, unfamiliar, she'd teach him, she thought
As she seductively behaved, his attention she caught.

She whispered sweet nothings and to the garden enticed
But, as midnight approached, with danger she diced
Disappearing before it was time to unmask
When he arrived home, she'd have questions to ask!

At 3 a.m., he returned home at last
To face many questions, she was to cast.
He reported the Ball, so dull had been
Without her beside him, it was not his scene!

So, with his mates to play poker instead he went,
Passed his costume to some philanderous gent.
She knew not who she'd enticed at the Ball
But it wasn't her dear husband, after all!

The Visit

The visit to the retirement home was a bit of a treat
Giving the chance for young and old to meet,
The old, to talk about times gone by
And the young, the flag of youth to fly.

One little girl approached a lady, her hand to hold
She asked her age and was proudly told
Ninety-eight years old and six months gone,
She wondrously asked, 'Did you start at one?'

Deep Shock!

The crevasse was deep, a long way down
As I listened to my companion, with a frown.
Nonchalantly, he was telling how his mountain guide
Fell down it last time – shock I could not hide.

'Just like that, you tell me without concern
How could you? I find it hard to discern.'
'It was only an old one,' he turned to say,
'There were several pages missing, anyway!'

Body Under the Stairs!

Finding a body under the stairs
I was taken completely unawares,
From where it came, I did not know
For me, it was an awful blow!

I'd never seen anything this dead before
It was very stiff, on the lino floor.
The body, I knew, I'd need help to remove
The longer it was left, it would not improve!

Soon I'd have officers crawling everywhere
Searching for clues, laying my house bare,
Trying to establish all they needed to know
I was shaking, with fear, from head to toe.

They'd want answers to questions they would ask,
While dealing with this horrendous task
My mind was a blur, I could not think straight
I was working myself into a terrible state!

I dialled the number, my request to make
Someone must come, the body to take
Rest I could not, until it had left the house,
'Pest control, I've found a dead mouse!'

The Burglar

He'd broken a window to gain access within
With no qualms about committing this sin,
He cared not of the mess he made
As he carried out his heartless raid.

Drawers were upturned, the contents tipped
Furniture damaged and curtains ripped
Ornaments broken, light fittings smashed
Everything in sight, he recklessly trashed.

His target was cash, jewellery too,
Some electrical items, to name but a few!
When he was done, he left with his haul
Escaping, unseen, over the garden wall.

Calling the police, on their shocking discovery,
The occupants were anxious for full recovery
Of all that was stolen, the burglar must pay
For desecrating their house in this awful way.

The police were swift to progress the case
As they followed some leads, the burglar to trace,
They were soon to succeed and caught up with him
He scratched his head, his expression was grim.

'I thought I was careful and very clever
No one could have seen my sly endeavour,
But where to find me, how did you know?'
'We followed your footprints in the snow!'

All for a Jag!

Jonathon was eccentric, he didn't trust banks
For their services, he was not in the ranks,
He worked very hard, stashed cash in hoards
Hidden away, under creaking floor boards.

He'd never had a problem in dealing this way
Just took what he needed, in order to pay
Cash from the floor boards, to settle his accounts
Whether it be small or large amounts.

This day he was buying a brand new car
With his heart set on a Jaguar,
Top of the range, he needed lots of cash
To the garage, with his notes, he prepared to dash.

Hundreds of notes he'd gathered together
Not taking account of the windy weather,
Outside the garage, all were blown from his hand
Raining fifty-pound notes, all over the land.

Passers-by and motorists couldn't believe their eyes
Scrambling for notes, as they fell from the skies.
Jonathon was stunned as he watched the attack
Knowing much of his money he'd never get back!

As he drove from the garage in his brand new car
Disappointed it wasn't a Jaguar
For not trusting banks, he had rued the day
The price of a Fiat was all he could pay!

Eyesight Foresight

As I look to the future, it is clear to me
That soon my eyes no longer will see,
My sight is failing, as each year passes
As another goes by, I need stronger glasses.

The newspaper print is shrinking for sure
As I squint to read a little more,
But soon the words will blur into one
My reading days will then be gone.

Threading a needle used to be easy going
Soon I'll have to abandon my sewing,
For, when the needle, I try to thread
My eyes won't function in my head.

Shopping can a nightmare be
As labels play a trick on me,
I pick up marmalade, it's really jam
The salmon tin when home, is Spam.

So you see, it's looking ever clear
That blindness must be very near,
Signs of old age, catching up with me
But then, I'm all of forty-three!

Tasty Oysters!

The restaurant was full, the attraction was clear
Topless waitress service was the fascination here.
The two men ogled, as they ordered their meal
The restaurant, to them, had special appeal!

The first man ordered tasty fresh oysters to eat
His partner could see they were in for a treat,
Served one-by-one, he insisted, twelve journeys in all
Ensuring the dish was enjoyed at each service call!

Jelly Melee!

The lady was complaining angrily in the chemist's store
She'd used contraceptive jelly over a month or more,
But now she was pregnant, she came to say
The jelly was useless, the chemist must pay.

Stocked near the food, she'd got confused
And ate it on toast, the product abused.
'No wonder you're pregnant,' the chemist turned white,
'If you'd read the directions, you'd have got it right!'

The Sofa Bed

The sofa bed had special appeal
Thickly padded and soft to the feel,
On it, young Dennis, with toys, would play
Listen to stories, or drowsily lay.

Until one day he got in a tight fix
While performing some of his usual tricks,
He threw himself on it and over did roll
When suddenly, and savagely, it swallowed him whole!

He banged and he thumped, but he couldn't get out
His mother came running when she heard him shout
But the sofa bed wouldn't give up its catch
And Dennis's mother was too weak a match.

The springs had closed up ever so tight
Dennis, inside, got quite a fright,
It was dark and he was afraid
To rescue him, came the fire brigade!

They cut up the sofa bed, to gain his release
Mutilated this offending furniture piece.
They suggested, in future, Dennis, with his toys
Should avoid sofa beds that swallow young boys!

Overheard

The conversation, they should not have heard
But they could hear every single word.
A voice was asking, 'Is it in?'
As they sat on the wall, with a grin!

Their next door neighbour was not alone
The voice they heard, to them, was unknown.
As she said, 'Just a bit further, nearly there,'
Their eyes widened, at each other to stare!

'Push some more, it's very tight!'
Came the voice, then sheer delight
'It's in, well done!' they heard her say
What were they doing? It was only midday.

Then, 'Now again, try some more
Push, that's good, now on to the floor'
Minutes later, the Chiropodist appeared
Slippers replaced and suspicion cleared!

Pasty Poser!

A student nurse, far from home, was I
When taking a break, a visitor drew nigh
A pasty, she offered, it was one of the best
'Could you possibly 'eat it?' was her request.

Tasty, it was, and not a difficult task
But the woman returned a little while later to ask,
'It seems t' be takin' a long time, pet
Is me 'usband's pasty 'ot enough yet?'

The Identity Parade

The lady was robbed several weeks before
The thief, she hoped, was in the hands of the law,
For an identity parade she must undertake
In an effort to expose this unscrupulous snake!

She walked the line of unsavoury men
Inspecting each one once, then looked again,
As a man in the line-up stepped out to shout
'It's her I robbed, without a doubt!'

The Babysitters

Helen was going out for the very first time,
After having her baby – it felt like a crime.
Ben was only a few weeks old
But she knew he'd be as good as gold.

Two sisters were babysitting for just an hour or two,
Helen had left instructions to make a brew.
They could have a sandwich while she was away
Ben was just fed, asleep he should stay.

So out Helen went with a friend until ten
Leaving the girls to watch over Ben,
They had a sandwich and made some tea
Ben slept right through, good was he.

On her return, Helen offered the girls a drink
As she went to the fridge, her heart did sink,
She couldn't tell them, but she could see
They'd used Ben's breast milk in their tea!

Air Sea Rescue

A difficult mission, no time to waste
Red alert – they must make haste.
The helicopter, with brave men on board
Took to the air, as engines roared.

A young man in difficulty on turbulent seas,
The temperature falling by several degrees.
The winter cold would complicate their goal
But they were each confident of their role.

Now the craft was positioned for rescue to commence
The men all knew these moments were tense,
As they hovered above the stricken man below
Was he alive or dead? They did not know!

Motionless he lay on upturned dinghy keel
His rescuer was lowered on life-line to kneel
With difficulty, as they swayed to and fro,
He managed the harness to fasten, then upward go.

Up and up the inert body was winched
And into the helicopter he was gently inched
He was cold and unconscious, but still alive,
With care and attention he would survive.

Congratulating themselves on a job well done
The team had accomplished a successful run
They'd rescued their man, safe and sound
The helicopter circled, homeward bound.

But fate, for the man, struck an extraordinary blow
As his harness was removed, the craft hit air flow
Which caused it to tilt, the injured man to ditch,
He fell to his death – oh life is a bitch!

A Lady's Pride

It happened in the fifties, when in her teens
Life was fun, exploring bright city scenes.
Boys were a new feature, in her life
It was on a date, when came her strife!

Shirley was queuing at the movies, with her new beau
When she felt the elastic in her knickers go,
Mortified, she was, as she felt them slip
Down to her ankles, they'd lost their grip!

Unnoticed by anyone, including her beau
She rescued the knickers, perched on her toe.
She lifted her foot and grabbed the tag
Then quickly she shoved them into her bag.

This operation complete, and no one aware
She knew there'd be no cause to stare,
She'd manage that night, with no underwear
No one would guess her bottom was bare!

Unfortunately, for her, the movie was sad
As she probed in her bag, for the hanky she had,
Out came the knickers, and without a thought
The tears she wiped, but this time was caught!

Shirley's beau looked over, his eyes a brim
But not from sadness, far from grim,
His laughter echoed loudly in her ear
His amusement was most obviously clear!

Nowadays, this dilemma would not occur
No more to cause an embarrassing stir,
For knicker elastic has been modified
The true saviour of a lady's pride!

Deep Within

Everyone's out, to church they've gone
The door is closed, the latch is on,
The house is quiet there's no one in
All is still from deep within.

The spider, her web, she quietly spins
The cat pulls wool from knitting pins
The dog's curled up by the fire asleep
The hamster from his nest does peep.

A fly, above them, on the ceiling, high
Watches all that passes by,
Mice scamper too, as beetles stray
About the house, this holy day.

Did someone say there's no one in
That all is still from deep within?
Why, that's untrue, God's creatures roam
Behind closed doors, they're all at home!

The Debt Collector

The debt collector was coming to call
They were hard up, there was no money at all,
When he knocked, a little girl answered the door
It was not his concern that they were poor.

The little girl looked up at the stern ugly man
She was frightened, her face was wan,
'Sorry, my mum's out, she's not in today
She's hiding in the coal shed, out the back way!'

Jammy Dodgers!

My family all love biscuits, I buy them every week
My biscuit tins, I fill, until they all but creak,
With custard creams near screaming, as I cram them in
Jammy dodgers dodging, as they are squeezed within!

Oozing tasty shortbread and some fruit and nut
My biscuit tins all bulging, the lids will hardly shut.
So, why is it when I come home and crave a tasty bite
My tins are always empty, with not a crumb in sight?

Who-Dun-It?

The book was outstanding, a very good read
With many characters who could be guilty indeed,
An enthralling mystery, Lord Don was dead
Who murdered the peer, found in his bed?

Was it the doctor, with no alibi?
Or the butler, who on whisky was high?
Could the maid have poisoned his drink?
Or was it the vicar, so low did sink?

Ample opportunity the housekeeper had
And the gardener admitted he'd been mad,
Angry at the victim, could he have erred?
Or was it the cook, as his tea she stirred?

The book was so gripping, I couldn't put it down
But when nearly finished, I was to grimace and frown,
Never to know who poisoned Lord Don
For the very last page in the book was gone!

Eric's Rabbit

Little Eric was holding his pet rabbit tight
Saying, 'Come on, Bunny, I know you're bright
Tell me the sum of two plus nine,
I know you can do it – just give me a sign!'

Eric's dad appeared, to hear his son
The rabbit's reaction was precisely none,
Perplexed that Eric should expect anything more
His dad came and sat with him on the floor.

'Rabbits can't do maths,' he gently explained,
Eric was indignant, his voice was strained.
'Rabbits multiply quickly, that's what my teacher said
But stupid Bunny can't even add up instead!'

Clever and Quiet

He was so clever, he couldn't be told
I was quiet, my tongue I'd hold
In borrowed car, a motorist's pride
I went along, just for the ride.

We started for home at the end of the day
Stopped to refuel, along the way,
Filled with petrol, we continued along
Until something with the car went drastically wrong!

It started to slow, splutter and croak
As the engine died with a seeming choke
He, being clever, would soon fix it he said,
But the car wouldn't go, the engine was dead.

Me, being quiet, I didn't say a word
But I was suspicious, to me it occurred,
That he'd put petrol where diesel should go
But I wouldn't tell him, for he should know!

Digitally Perfect

My bathroom scales seemed past their day
Old they were, not much longer to stay,
I'd been slimming, to lose some extra pounds
So heavy, I was, they made creaking sounds.

For over a month, the scales had read
The very same weight, though I'd underfed
No good were these, if I were to keep a tab
On the progress I was making, losing the flab!

So I treated myself to the best scales indeed
Top of the range, accuracy guaranteed,
Digitally perfect, I could be well assured
They would truthfully tell how well I'd scored.

But my new scales were to give me an almighty shock
The very first time, it was as if they did mock
Registering the same old weight, my ego to dent
The only pounds lost were those I had spent!

Where is It?

His wife was constantly moving the furniture about
He'd get frustrated when he was in doubt
Never able to find things from one week to the next
Which left him, so often, very cross and vexed.

This night was no exception, when asleep in bed
Someone knocked on the door, up he sped,
Half-awake, he ran into the dark living-room
There hitting a wall, with a very loud boom.

His wife awoke when she heard the sound
Of his very cross voice, she worriedly frowned,
He shouted to her, as he lay on the floor,
'Now where have you put the wretched front door?'

On Campus

A student on campus was amazed when his mate
Rode up on a bike, proud and sedate,
'How did you get that?' he asked in awe
Knowing his mate was financially poor.

He told of a young lady on campus last night
Who stopped on her bike, and to his delight
She took everything off, saying, 'Take what you like'
Her clothes did not fit, so he took her bike!

My Parrot

My parrot is no talker, in fact he's very quiet
Though next door's never stops, it really is a riot.
I asked them to divulge, the secret of their success
How they made their parrot talk and everyone impress?

They did not know the answer, it was very clear to me
Their parrot is a talker, quite naturally, you see,
Mine must have a complex, to never say a word
They said I should not hesitate and get another bird.

But I could not be disloyal, I've had him since a boy
But am very disappointed that my parrot is so coy,
I've tried all that I could think of to make him speak to me
But never can I coax a word, forever quiet is he.

He sits quite still on his perch as if he knows I mind
That he doesn't talk to me, though I'm always very kind.
There's no point in being angry, or getting very huffed
When my parrot cannot speak, because he's only stuffed!

Dog in Disgrace!

In the kitchen we stood; me, my son and his gran
A delicious aroma emitting from the cooking pan,
Lunch would soon be ready, even the dog was aware
As he stood wagging his tail, with his nose in the air.

Suddenly, all became aware of an unwelcome smell
The kind not discussed, but recognised well,
Gran took the broom as she screwed up her face
The dog was in trouble – he was in disgrace!

'You smelly dog!' exclaimed poor Gran,
She waved her broom, as out he ran
My son looked on with a smile on his face
At the sight of Gran and the dog in disgrace.

Normality returned with the dog excluded
Lunch was eaten and the visit concluded
On the way home, my son giggled and said,
'Mum, the dog didn't do it – I did it instead!'

The Airport Bus

The airport bus on the tarmac was ready
As the old gent's daughter held him steady,
Mounting the bus, the stewardess was heard to say,
'Welcome aboard, we're now on our way.'

On asking the old man what he thought so far
His daughter felt her mouth fall ajar
When he replied, as he scratched his jaw,
'I've never seen one without wings before!'

The Wedding!

The groom has an iron railing wrapped around his neck
The best man's lost the ring, the bride's a nervous wreck,
The bridesmaids are all sobbing, their hair has gone awry
The pageboy's pulling faces, the organist's too high!

The ushers are confused, they cannot get it right
The bride's mother's hat is a nauseating sight.
The vicar's lost for words, he's praying on his knees
The flowers in the church make the choir sneeze.

The wedding now is over, despite what's gone before
Forced to spend their wedding night on the bedroom floor,
The bed, you see, collapsed, the last of many straws
No more can they take, so they're filing for divorce!

Emergency Call

Brenda rang the fire brigade, an emergency to report
The alarm raised, they followed procedure, as taught,
With sirens blaring, they responded so fast
As to the notified address they hurriedly dashed.

They knew this mission was going to be tough
For all involved, it would surely be rough,
But they were professionals, used to all manner of work
Trained to cope, their duty never to shirk.

Eight firemen arrived with the greatest of speed
As Brenda waited, the way to lead
To the back door, where, stuck very tight
Was her dog, in the cat flap, barking in fright!

Jim Wrote...

Jim wrote a letter to his dad, pleading his return
To see him once again, he really had a yearn
He'd now been gone two weeks, Jim was missing him
Without his dad around, life was really grim.

Jim wrote, 'Dad, please come home, we miss you very
    much
Your smile, your jokes around the house, your very special
    touch,
Being a single parent my mum just cannot cope
My sisters want you back again, all day they sit and mope!'

Jim wrote in his neatest hand, so Dad would be impressed
Signed it with his love, and the envelope addressed,
He did it all himself, though he was only seven
Then he took it to the pillar-box and posted it to Heaven.

The Berk

'My anti-perspirant roll-on does not work,'
Complained the man, who was quite a berk,
'My body odour, it does not prevent
I really am still a smelly gent!'

This man's concern, his mate could not understand
For roll-ons usually satisfied demand,
The berk explained the roll-on caused him pain
And he would not be using it ever again.

His mate questioned how it could have this effect
He himself never had trouble, he could reflect
'The instructions, I followed,' the berk's voice was curt,
'*Remove lid and push up bottom* – ooh how it hurt!'

Legal Sport!

A crime committed, the finger pointed
Accusations made, witnesses appointed,
Legal aid rejected, expected guilty to plead
What kind of example is this to lead?

The poor can't be innocent, is that what they think?
Why does the system positively stink?
No one to advise or help in this case
The prosecution loaded, the defence a disgrace.

They won't stand for it, they'll fight to the end
Justice to seek, innocence to defend
For proper defence one has every right,
A solicitor will be present to put up a fight!

They'll beg and they'll borrow, but they won't steal
To defend this case which they strongly feel
Should have been resolved before going to court
No one really cares – it's just legal sport!

There's no guarantee that the case will be won
But they must conclude what the law has begun
Their faith in the judicial system remains very strong
It must establish his innocence, all along!

Of course, someone knows he didn't commit
This crime for which they must surely acquit
This someone was responsible, for the crime, you see
He couldn't have done it, for it was me!

Stag Night Stabbing

It was the last day in March, as midnight struck
When Andrew had a terrible change of luck
He'd hosted a party, had too much to drink
When he stepped outside, he felt himself sink.

Into oblivion, his mind wandered far away
As he missed the next few hours of the day,
When he awoke, his surroundings he scanned
Shocked to find a blood-stained knife in his hand.

He was aware of police officers everywhere
A body beside him, he had to stare
What had he done, while in a drunken state?
The man on the ground had been his best mate!

He was taken away to sit in a cell
He was cold and hungry, feeling unwell
What would they do to him, for killing his mate
How much longer would he have to wait?

It had been his stag party, the night before
Then, his life had been mapped out for sure
A wonderful girl he was soon to wed
Now his whole future hung by a thread!

It was 8 a.m. when the cell door opened wide
Andrew looked in surprise as his 'dead mate', he spied.
Smiling, he was, and looking smugly cool,
'Andrew,' he laughed, 'it was an April Fool!'

First Love

Our daughter is in love for the very first time
She's still quite young, he's in his prime,
Every spare minute, together they share
For him, she says, she'll always be there.

Homework gets done at the very last minute
If she had her own way, she'd probably bin it
For schoolwork she finds onerous and grim
She's only happy, when she's with him.

She misses her meals, Dad gets cross
But to know where she is, he's not at a loss,
She's gone to snatch some time with him
When she feels the need she's off on a whim.

We went away for Christmas and New Year
She missed him so much, she shed a tear,
Counting the hours when together they'd be
Time spent apart is such agony.

We pray to God, she doesn't get hurt
Or fall on her face, in the dirt.
Maxine's only eleven, but this love isn't phoney,
His name is Fizz, her beloved pony!

Stan

There was a man called Stan
Who had a fetish for eating bran,
He regularly ate
A very full plate
Which made Stan a regular man!

The Gambler

There was a big gambler called Mel
Who lost his house to Jimmy Bell,
'Winner takes all,'
He was heard to call
'You can take the wife as well!'

Brian's Watch

Brian's watch was special – it played a tune
Always at midnight, again at noon
Wherever it was, on or off his wrist
This tune it played, it never missed.

He wore it when he went fishing at sea
As it played the tune, his mates laughed with glee,
For they'd never seen such a watch before
As they cast their lines for fish galore.

Then a mishap occurred, as his line grew taut
A struggle ensued, with the fish he'd caught,
It broke his strap, the watch was lost
As into the sea it was haplessly tossed.

The men watched as they saw it gracefully sink
Then something happened to make them blink
A fish swam by and swallowed it whole
Brian was upset and hard to console.

Brian's watch, at noon, was found weeks later
By a chef, preparing the fish, to cater,
Startled he was and ran from the room
The fish on the slab was playing a tune!

Early Morning Alarm

The alarm awoke me, I gave it a bash
It was time to rise, I had to dash,
Showered and dressed, the kettle on
I roused the children, one by one.

The bacon sizzled, as they got dressed
Shiny shoes and school shirts pressed,
I packed their bags, dinner money too
Opened the curtains and made a brew!

The darkness was depressing, this winter's morn
Still half asleep, I stifled a yawn,
The children bickered, as breakfast they ate
This morning ritual, I could truly hate.

Next came the mad bathroom rush
Their faces to wash and teeth to brush
A comb through tangled and dishevelled hair
'At last!' I sighed, 'we're nearly there!'

I glanced at the clock to avoid any fuss
Or chance they had of missing the bus,
I couldn't believe my eyes when I saw
The time was only half past four.

'Oh, Mum,' they cried, 'what have you done?
You know getting up is not much fun
We're off back to bed, the right time to return
How to set the alarm, will you ever learn?'

Katie's Kitten

A beautiful bundle of tiny fluff
Snuggled up to Katie's cuff,
'I'll call her Sophie,' she said with glee
As she lovingly held her on her knee.

A pink ribbon she bought for her cute pet
And showed her off to all she met
So proud she was of her new friend
Prime time together they would spend.

Sophie's favourite meal was fish
Eaten from her special dish
With fancy letters on the side
Displaying Sophie's name with pride.

Katie was the envy of the neighbourhood
For Sophie was cute and very good
Her friends were always coming to call
To play with Sophie, loved by all!

'One day when she's fully grown
She'll have kittens of her own,'
Said Katie, 'What I plan to do
Is give a kitten to each of you.'

When Katie took Sophie to the vet
It was a day she would never forget.
'This pink ribbon looks bonny,' his voice was coy,
'But, she's a he – it's blue for a boy!'

In Swarms

A swarm of mosquitoes attacked two campers one night
As they dived under canvas to escape their plight
Later emerging, they were most thankful to see
The mosquitoes had gone, at last they were free!

They saw, minutes later, from where they lay
A flight of fire flies heading their way,
'We're in for it now, wait for the bites
They're coming to find us with little spotlights!'

Two Monkeys

The lorry driver had two monkeys on his load
When a breakdown occurred, on the southbound road
A young man duly stopped and offered to assist
He'd take the monkeys to the zoo, indeed he did insist.

The lorry driver was grateful for his help in this way
The monkeys were in safe hands, the young man he did
    say,
So off he went with the monkeys, to the Parkland Zoo
Leaving the lorry driver, awaiting breakdown crew!

When repairs were all completed, he continued on his way
The zoo, his destination, to check the monkey bay,
To ensure they were both safe, and duly settled in
Two monkeys, in their new home, snug and warm within.

But, as he neared the entrance, he had a big surprise
For there was the young man, he could not believe his eyes,
With two monkeys, hand in hand, they'd visited the zoo
Now destined for the cinema, a movie to view!

Youth of Today!

The youth walked purposefully into the corner shop
Earring dangling and shaved hair crop,
Tattooed, with nose-stud shining bright
Enough to give decent folk a fright.

Warily, the assistant watched as he approached
She was serving a pensioner when he encroached
He looked at the lady and cheekily declared,
'Hurry up, Granny!' The assistant glared.

'How dare you speak to my customer that way
There is no respect from the youth of today.
You wait your turn, as you always should
To be rude to people will do you no good!'

The pensioner, unable to believe her ears
Could not understand the assistant's jeers,
Bemused, she said, 'Now have you done?
I *am* his granny – he's my daughter's son!'

Seven out of Ten!

The weather at the airport was atrociously bad
The pilot, circling above, was getting quite mad,
Though calmly, on the intercom, he confidently spoke
Trying to soothe all the passenger folk.

'Conditions are bad, I have to say
But seven out of ten planes made it today.'
After a deathly hush, from the passenger bay
He added, 'The others were diverted another way!'

Lamb Jam!

Sam was four, a visiting city kid
Out in the country, watching the farmer's bid
To help a ewe give birth to a lamb,
It was obvious to him it was in a tight jam.

The farmer proficiently helped it on its way
As he brought it to rest on some welcoming hay
He gave it a sharp slap, a breath it took
Bleated loudly, as Sam came closer to look.

He then stood with his hands on his hips
As he chided the lamb through smiling lips,
'You naughty little thing, were you insane?
Don't you ever get yourself in that fix again!'

Hitch-Hike!

A hard day's work finished and done
The mile walk home would not be fun,
Impulsively, I decided to hitch-hike that day
An elderly couple then drove my way.

As they stopped the car on the kerb side
I jumped in the back for my homeward ride,
For stopping, I thanked them, most gratefully
They looked at each other and smiled at me.

They asked my address and drove me all the way
I wondered at their kindness to me that day,
But, was mortified, on asking if they lived far
To hear home was where I got in the car!

The Cat

The cat was curious, he'd never before seen
A cricket match on the village green,
He stood by the pavilion to watch and eye
The players as they batted the ball up high.

He moved in nearer for a closer view
As his curiosity grew and grew,
Mick was standing ready to bat the ball
Took a hard swing, wasn't close at all.

The bat left his hand, flew through the air
Landing on the cat, standing there,
Flattened, he was, under the cricket bat
Curiosity killed the unfortunate cat.

Deafening Silence

It's hard to convey messages, when you've lost your voice
You have to write notes – you have no choice,
Even that can be difficult, with a scrawl like mine
When trying to communicate with a boy of nine.

With chores to be done, my voice was no better
I signalled to my son to post a letter,
That, he understood, but I also wanted some cheese
Over my writing he stumbled, saying, 'Print it please!'

In bold loud letters, I printed clear and good
Immediately he nodded, he understood,
Calling back cheekily, as he went out
'Mum, you really do not have to shout!'

Sweet Passion

His jacket on the bedpost, socks beneath the chair
Shoes upturned, just cast aside, left without a care
Shirt tossed on the wardrobe, tie hanging on the door
Her stockings on the light-shade, their undies on the floor.

Her blouse, haplessly discarded, skirt abandoned too
His once neatly pressed trousers, lying creased and all
    askew,
Two bodies all entwined, their room an utter mess
Wrapped in love's sweet passion, they couldn't care much
    less.

Until morning brought their young son, bursting through
    the door
Wide-eyed, exclaiming loudly, at the shocking sight he saw,
'Mum and Dad, I think you should practice what you
    preach
And keep your bedroom tidy – the rules you should not
    breach!'

Duly Noted!

After a tiff with her husband, they ceased to speak
Silence descended, neither were weak,
With a hair appointment booked for early next day
She wished him to wake her, but just couldn't say.

So leaving him a note, off to bed she stomped
Having requested he wake her at 7.30 prompt,
The tiff then forgotten, she slept like a log
Until woken at 8.30, by the family dog.

Her husband had left for work long before
Not bothering to wake her, as her note did implore
But, on the pillow beside her, he'd left neatly pinned
A note saying 'Wake Up' which she angrily binned!

Quick to Learn!

The visitor was foreign, no English he knew
To learn the language, he was anxious to do,
To assist with this, he carried everywhere
A dictionary, to which he would often refer.

This day, in the park, he was taking a stroll
It was quiet and peaceful, good for the soul,
He'd recline on a bench and enjoy the fresh air
While he checked the words on the notice near there.

He took from his pocket the reference book
But before he'd even had a chance to look,
He was quick to learn what the notice conveyed
'Wet Paint' were the words, and in it he laid!

Phobic Fear

It was the biggest one she'd ever seen
Looking dark and hairy and very mean
She could hardly face this ugly sight
Terrified, and filled with fright.

It signified danger, to one so green
Young and nervous, only seventeen
But it was time, her fear to overcome
As grown up, she would soon become.

Her mother had warned her to be on her guard
But she found it irksome and very hard
Coming to terms, along this path
When facing a spider in the bath!

Returning Jo!

She stood before him in the road ahead
He braked sharply and stopped quite dead,
His lights caught the features of a pretty young girl
His heart beat fast, his mind in a whirl.

He helped her to the car, she was clearly lost
Trembling all over, her body cold as frost,
She told him her name, that she yearned for home
Pleaded he take her, no longer to roam.

He turned his car and followed Jo's lead
Serene she looked now, he was fulfilling her need
They stopped in her driveway, he heard her sigh
Alighted the car, to the doorstep drew nigh.

Jo's mother opened the door, looking expectantly at him
Her eyes were tearful, her countenance was grim
He turned to escort Jo safely to her mum
But she'd disappeared, he was rendered quite numb!

Her mother thanked him for his kindness this night
Her voice was calm, as she shed some light,
Her daughter, she explained, died this day, years ago
He was the ninth young man to return her Jo.

The Runners

The runners were at the start
Waiting for the gun to impart
The race was on
Then they'd be gone
But they'd soon be back at the start!

I Wonder

I wonder what people see
Through their eyes, when they look at me,
Do they see beauty and flair
True character there?
Or do they just see little old me!

Tamagotchi Crazy!

A Tamagotchi is an electronic pet
Hand-held menace, with battery set,
The latest trend of children everywhere
A living nightmare – parents beware!

The button pressed, their pet is born
Parents view this, with positive scorn
Knowing full well the attention it needs
Craving constant care and regular feeds.

They have to accommodate its every whim
If they don't, the consequences are grim
It makes a noise, they have to comply
They cannot ignore it, or it will die.

They become attached, it goes everywhere
To bed, to school, for constant care
There is no let up, wherever they are
As it travels with them, near and far.

But the sting comes when its welcome has vanished
Expelled from school, its presence is banished
A disturbing influence, it has to be left behind
With reluctant parents, to nurture and mind!

The Butcher's Con

Ellis was a butcher of wide repute
A businessman, and very cute.
A lady walked into his shop one day,
'A chicken please, Butcher, if I may!'

'I've got one at three pounds ten ounces here
It's cheap enough, a bargain, dear!'
The lady looked, 'Do you have a bigger one?'
The butcher then performed a con!

For this was the only chicken he had in store
The rest were sold, he had no more
So he returned the chicken to the counter below
Then shoved it further along the row.

Unbeknown to the lady, he brought the same one out
With his thumb on the scale, it was heavier, no doubt,
'It's your lucky day, the price has been cut
I'd like it sold, before we shut!'

The lady, a bargain she could not resist
Thanked the butcher for being able to assist,
'As your prices are so very keen
I'll buy both the chickens I have seen!'

Bink's Wink

There was a boy called Bink
Who was trying hard to wink
But his eyes wouldn't play
Together they'd stay
His wink was only a blink!

The Sculptor

There was a sculptor called Hugh
Whose work three young men came to view,
'That's not a bust,'
They said, in disgust,
'There's only head and shoulders on view!'

The Briefcase

The briefcase he held tightly and would not let go
The contents of which, they were intrigued to know
They suspected it could be drugs in the case he had
A bomb, or something as dangerous and bad!

Though, in trouble, he had never been before
He'd always stayed on the right side of the law,
He was acting suspicious, they were determined to see
The contents of the briefcase he held on his knee.

They'd had a tip-off from a lady he knew
But of the contents, she had no clue,
Though sure she was he carried something wrong
Her opinions on this had been very strong.

He'd acted so cagey when she'd only enquired,
Of his unusual attachment to the case she was tired
The contents he would not reveal, to her least of all
So she'd decided her option was the police to call.

They were now ready to pounce on their quarry
But they were going to be embarrassed, and sorry
For the man was to show them he had a perfect right
To carry in his briefcase what was in it that night!

Friday the Thirteenth

Ted rang his boss, just to say,
'I cannot come to work today
It's Friday the thirteenth, unlucky for me
I'm not tempting fate, you must agree!'

His long-suffering wife, whom he loved dear
Made her opinion very clear,
'What will happen, will be your fate
Now I must be off, or I'll be late!'

Back in bed, he was feeling calm
Thinking he was safe from harm
The ceiling then fell down on his head
Yes, Friday the thirteenth was grim for Ted!

Early Start!

His job required a very early start
As he rose each day, he hadn't the heart
To disturb his wife, for later so busy she'd be
With their three young children to oversee.

Many times when he'd left, one of the children would
    creep
In quietly beside her, and fall asleep
One morning, she awoke to the sound of the phone,
She answered 'Hello,' in a sleepy tone.

His boss was asking if her husband had left for work
That morning, her answer would cause him to smirk
For, she said, 'I'll check,' still groggy and dim,
'Someone's lying beside me – I'll see if it's him!'

Teacher's Marks

For the mark within a circle, I had a look
It was the teacher's style, when marking a book,
This particular occasion, I'd struggled to apply
Myself to the task, although I did try.

I was reluctant to see what mark I'd scored
For it wasn't a subject in which I soared,
I felt I'd done the best I possibly could
But had reason to doubt my effort was good.

Though the circle was there, the teacher had erred
Forgotten the mark inside – I had a word,
He assured me the mark was there, and it hurt
It was the circle outside, he'd failed to insert!

Knife Happy

The knife he used was sharp and thin
He felt no guilt as the blade went in
Piercing skin and flesh beneath
His face set hard, with gritted teeth.

Then, with cutting thrusts, he commenced dissection
Deftly slicing in each direction
When he was finished, he smiled with glee
As he wiped the knife upon his knee.

Disposal next was on his mind
As the pieces in a row he lined
The result of his efforts all complete
Now his apple was ready to eat!

On Safari

The safari park was a thrilling place
With wonder expressed on the little girl's face
Many animals she'd seen that exciting day
But the giraffe was elusive, to her dismay.

Unbeknown to her, he was closer than she knew
As she walked ahead, seeking a positive view,
Under his tail, along the length of his belly
Between front legs, then she quivered like jelly.

She looked up skyward and finally spied
The head of the giraffe, held high with pride
She whooped with excitement still blissfully unaware
She was under the body, of the giraffe up there!

Dark Terror!

He walked through the cemetery an eerie place
It was dark, he was frightened and quickened his pace,
He could hear a tap, tap, tapping sound
Which convinced him evil was all around.

His fright became terror, as louder it grew
Until, suddenly, a man came into view,
Crouched low, he could see, he was chiselling away
At a gravestone, which in front of him lay.

Relieved, he was, to see another man there
No longer frightened, with company to share,
But he was soon to run off, wailing loud and long
When told by the man, 'My name is spelt wrong!'

A Fond Farewell

The occasion was a most solemn affair
A tear in the eye of everyone there,
The congregation were all sombrely bedecked
Showing their sadness and utmost respect.

Their departed friend would have been proud
Of the service, the words, the hymns sung loud,
All proceedings conducted with dignity and grace
As tears trickled down each and every young face.

The burial over, they dried their eyes
Looking upward to heaven and darkening skies,
'Lord,' they prayed, 'please love and keep
Our cherished hamster, who died in his sleep!'

Instant Attraction!

She swept up beside him a beautiful creature
Tantalising him, with each perfect feature
His attraction was instant, he felt his pulse race
She was responding, a smile on her face.

He could not believe this was happening to him
His luck with the ladies was usually grim
She was different, on him focusing her eyes
He was her target, he gaped in surprise!

This fair lady was the answer to all his prayers
The one that most men would wish to be theirs,
She drew herself close and pressed her lips to his ear
'Your flies are undone!' her mission then clear!

Tyred Out!

My car needed a tyre change, sad to say
As I pulled on to the roadside, one fine day,
With tools from the boot anxious to proceed
I loosened the nuts, until the wheel was freed.

With the old wheel off, and lying on the ground
To the boot, for the replacement I was bound,
When a car stopped nearby, the driver alighted
He headed for the bonnet, looking delighted.

With his head bowed busily, I challenged him
How dare he? I gave him a look so grim
On asking his business, his reply was sublime,
'If you're having the tyres, the battery is mine!'

The Vicar's Recovery

The vicar had been unwell, he'd had to forsake
His parish for a while – he'd no choice to make
A hospital stay, then convalescence was needed
Vital for recovery, the doctors he'd heeded!

His parishioners all held their vicar most dear
News of his progress, they were anxious to hear,
Hoping he'd soon recover to continue his role
For his absence in the parish left a vacuum, a hole.

Now, with the vicar's recovery nearly fully complete
His return to the parish was an imminent treat,
The notice-board conveyed the news quicker than a letter
Under 'God is Good' was posted 'The vicar is better!'

Quiet Please!

A family arriving at a guest house one day
Was greeted by the landlady, who deigned to say,
'You must be quiet we do insist
From making a noise, you must resist!'

'You don't have a radio, with which to disturb?'
She asked, afraid others it might perturb.
'Your children aren't noisy?' She was quickly assured,
'And your dog doesn't bark?' Her questions they endured.

'You can be sure,' said her guest, 'my family are quiet
We have no intention of causing a riot
But I think I should mention that now and then
You may hear the odd scratch from my fountain pen!'

Tear-Jerker

She stood at the sink, with tears in her eyes
The knife was sharp, though small in size,
Poised for action to see her task through
Cutting her wrist, from which blood withdrew.

Still the tears poured in a constant flow
It would soon be over, her troubles would go
To finish this task was the only way,
'Why end it all?' I hear you say!

'Surely her troubles are not that bad,
Could all be sorted to make her glad?'
But to make it clear, her only troubles, I think
Are the onions she's slicing in the sink!

Thank God!

Enquired the little girl, 'Did God make me?'
'Of course He did,' said Mum, 'perfectly.'
'Did He make you too?' she then did ask
'Yes, He did, it was no mean task!'
'And Granny too,' the girl enquired
Her mother sighed, for she was tired.
'Yes, Granny too, now please your questions end
God made us all, do you comprehend?'
The little girl thought hard, then smiled with glee,
'Thank God, He'd improved when He made me!'

117

His Apple

He'd enjoyed his lunch, now he was full
As the stalk, on his apple, he started to pull
He'd not eat it now, but save it for later
When his hunger returned his apple would cater.

He caressed it and turned it round in his hand
Fondled it warmly against his gold wedding band,
Pressed it to his chest, in a deep-cleaning action
Gleaming now, and ripe, was his apple's attraction.

After all his effort though, a mishap befell
The apple left his hand, he'd be reluctant to tell,
On to the floor, it rolled, to gather all kinds of dirt
Next stop for his apple? His ill-fated shirt!

Butler Jim

'Butler, Butler, do you hear, I'm going out tonight
Take the evening off, I think that would be right,
Enjoy yourself, for I won't be back 'til late
Relax and take it easy,' suggested Lady Kate.

So Lady Kate went out, leaving Butler Jim
With free time on his hands, to follow any whim.
But Lady Kate returned much earlier than he thought
In her chair he was reclining, well and truly caught.

Upstairs, to her room, she beckoned Butler Jim
Locked the door, then smiled sweetly up at him.
She purred, 'Take off my dress,' this he carefully did,
'Now take off my undies.' He did as he was bid.

Tension now was mounting in this bedroom scene
Butler Jim was nervous, as Lady Kate turned mean,
Her words were to sting him. 'Butler, I insist
You do not wear my clothes again, or you will be
    dismissed!'

The Spinster

There was a spinster from Tyrone
Who was tired of being alone
So she placed an ad
Wed a bachelor lad
Now, with kids, she's never alone!

The Electrician

There was an electrician called Doc
Who got an electrical shock
It wasn't the fact
That the current attacked
It was the price of electrical stock!

Happy Day

I sprang from my bed, as day was dawning
The feeling was good, this lovely morning,
I was happy, the sun was shining bright
Everything today could only go right.

Breakfast eaten, I was ready to leave
I hummed a tune, as I adjusted my sleeve,
I looked in the mirror, my collar was straight
Now I was ready, I would not be late.

I whistled as to the bus stop I walked
With others, in the queue, I cheerily talked,
The bus duly arrived and I took my seat
The journey was pleasant, a real treat.

Soon I arrived at my place of work
Still feeling happy, full of perk,
This day was going to get even better
I had that feeling nothing could fetter.

As I started cheerfully on my first task
A colleague approached, a question to ask,
'Sorry, I'm sure this will ruin your day
Why are you wearing odd shoes today?'

The Interview

The interview was important, Jake was determined to
   succeed
He needed this position, from the dole to be freed,
He'd paid careful attention to the way he was dressed
Anxious that the theatre would be impressed!

When he arrived, he was greeted and asked
To take the stage for the very first task.
'Would you like to sing a song for us first?'
He knew he could have been better rehearsed!

So Jake sang a song, though he was rusty he knew
It was well received, his confidence grew,
Though he was surprised that this interview entailed
This depth of performance, not formerly detailed.

When it was over, he breathed a relieved sigh
He was shaking a little, his mouth was dry
He was thanked for attending, they'd let him know
In a few days time, if he'd star in the show.

Now Jake was surprised, 'Don't you need to see
The driving documents I've brought with me?
I feel there's been an awful mistake
It's the van driver's job, I'd like to take!'

Dawn's Scorn

There was a nurse called Dawn
A doctor she was heard to scorn,
'He knows not what
The patient has got
Even I can see it's a corn!'

Airport Agony

I was flying home, after a month away
Being met at the airport, later that day,
Excited I was, my boyfriend I'd see
I'd missed him so much; had he missed me?

Then came the moment at the flight end
To collect my luggage, through Customs wend,
To stand at our allotted meeting place
And wait for him to show his face.

I waited an hour, but he didn't appear
He'd abandoned me, it seemed quite clear,
Upset I was, he hadn't bothered to come
So that's how he felt, I was feeling numb.

Then came a message over the Tannoy,
'Calling a passenger, Miss Heather Roy,
Please come to Reception right away,
We have a call from Robert May.'

I hurried along dragging my luggage behind
When we spoke, I felt peace of mind,
He'd really missed me; and did I know!
For he was at Gatwick, I at Heathrow!

PC Farr

There was a PC called Farr
Who drove a panda car
Into a brick wall
Beyond duty's call
Too fast it was driven by Farr!

The Clown

There was a circus clown
Unhappy and feeling down
Though a smile he wore
The sadness one saw
In the tears on the face of the clown!

Stacked Up!

The paint cans were stacked up, ever so high
As I spotted the one I wanted to buy
Right at the top, of course, it had to be
With no one to help get it down for me.

I decided I would have to help myself
As I stacked up some cans from the lower shelf
Standing on them precariously, I wobbled about
Reached up for the can, but it toppled out!

Past me, it fell, so remarkably quick
Spilling out the paint, all creamy and thick,
The lid had come off, leaving the DIY store
With a red-faced shopper and paint on the floor.

I stepped down from my precarious perch
As the elusive assistant came in search
Of the cause of the scream that I had expelled,
And looked, in horror, at the mess he beheld.

He was to question why I'd been so dim
Precariously balanced, risking life and limb
Reaching up high for the paint myself
When there was a similar can on the bottom shelf!

Something and Nothing

Nothing, with money, was a careful lad
Something spent every penny he had
So Nothing had something
And Something had nothing
Between them something and nothing, they had!

Best Kept Secret

It was the best kept secret on the factory floor,
Nobody knew and nobody saw
That they were lovers, and colleagues too
Keeping their passion from public view!

They'd meet when they could in the office above
Snatching precious time to declare their love,
It was a private place and out of the way
Assured, they were, that their secret would stay.

Their friends and colleagues had no clue
For they kept their distance in public view,
So clever they were, that no one would guess
They were often to snatch a tender caress.

Then, one day, during one such rendezvous
Something happened, quite out of the blue
Their secret was out, the Tannoy was broadcasting
To the entire factory, their love chat was blasting.

Though they were sublimely unaware of this fact
Comprehension and understanding, they lacked,
That, in future, it was no longer to be
The best kept secret in the factory!

Fish Fancy

It was a fancy restaurant, they were in for a treat
The best fish diner – they could choose fresh to eat,
For all around them fish, lobsters and crabs
Were on magnificent show and up for grabs.

Sue and her friends were just selecting their starter
When she spotted a poor fish, though she was no martyr,
It was floundering, but she knew just what to do
As she took it from the water and close to it drew.

She massaged the fish, until it was considerably improved
At her action, her friends were impressively moved
They watched as she returned it to the tank,
For saving its life, the fish had Sue to thank.

Their starter arrived and they chatted as they ate
Sue watched the fish swimming, as she cleared her plate,
Then horrified she was, for another diner had craved
The fish, for his next course, that Sue had just saved.

No objections could they raise, though it was hard to take
They knew that the restaurant had a living to make,
They asked for the manager, he was duly found
Unable to face fish, they requested pizzas all round!

The Death of Jeremy Court

The police had come to report
The death of Jeremy Court,
'Oh no!' his mum cried
Sweeping her knitting aside,
'I've finished this sweater for naught!'

The Little Green Man

I awoke from my slumbers, to find by my bed
A little green man, with a funny shaped head,
He was looking at me with pain in his eyes
Should I sink below covers or gently rise?

He was not like anyone I'd ever seen before
His eyes protruded and beard fell to the floor
The long pointed ears and crooked nose, I spied
With hard, wrinkled skin, crusty and dried.

I decided he was friendly, I had nothing to fear
Though what he wanted was somewhat unclear
His high-pitched moans drew sympathy in me
I rose in my bed to crouch on one knee.

'What's the matter?' I asked, 'are you in pain?'
He sounded distressed, I looked closely again
Then I spotted the cause of his obvious alarm
As a shiny gold pin, I plucked from his arm.

Immediately he disappeared in a puff of smoke
Then rising in bed, from my dream I awoke,
'Little green men, in the night!' I laughed,
Grateful, indeed, I was not going daft.

I rose to greet the new day ahead
Fluffed the pillows and made the bed
Suddenly my heart beat faster within
For there, on the floor, was a shiny gold pin!

Grandad's Mirror

The mirror had been precious a long time ago
But now all it signified was sadness and woe,
It had been Ian's grandad's pride and joy
Given to him when just a small boy.

As it was old, tarnished and past its best
Ian had laid it in an old wooden chest
After Grandad willed it into his care
Saying he hoped he'd see fortune in there.

'One's face is one's fortune,' he used to say,
'If you look in this mirror every day
Your fortune you will see in there
A reflection, true and always fair!'

But fortune, to Ian, had never come his way
The mirror was too shabby to have on display
Hence the chest had become its resting place
Wrapped in an old tablecloth, of lace.

Then Ian's daughter, Emma, found it there
Took off the cloth and laid it bare,
She liked the mirror, when restoring it she saw
Not just her reflection, much, much more.

Grandad had been right, there was a fortune in there
Money stashed inside, with clever flair,
They could face the future, he'd been right to tell
Grandad's mirror reflected their fortune well!

Daisy the Donkey

There was a farmer's old donkey called Daisy
Who was stubborn and very lazy
The farmer though inventive
Could find no incentive
Only a bomb could have uprooted his Daisy!

Russian Roulette

It was a game that could not be won
With five empty chambers in the gun,
The sixth held the fatal bullet within
To play this game was a mortal sin.

One of them would soon be dead
Shot with a bullet through the head
Administered by his own fair hand
As the rules, laid down, demand.

A lady was the reason for this act
Together they'd made this deadly pact,
For only one could win this prize
The other would suffer sad demise.

As the barrel spun round and round
In the room, there was no sound
Would the first shot be the one
To signify the prize was won?

The trigger was pulled, the first shot released
But the man with the gun was not deceased,
Now he passed it to the second man
Beads of sweat, down his face they ran.

The second shot ended in a click,
Again it hadn't done the trick,
A sigh of relief was loudly expelled
He was still alive, had not been felled.

The third and fourth shots were duly triggered
Without the result that both men figured,
But when the fifth shot echoed very loud
The noise soon drew a curious crowd.

They found one man shot in the head
The other, the heart, both were dead.
The bullet had ricocheted and killed the pair
So, neither won the lady fair!

Gardener Ray

There was a gardener called Ray
Who talked to his plants every day
They grew so big
He'd to build a rig
To climb for a chat every day!

The Bird-Watcher

The bird-watcher sat in his brand new hide
Designed and made, by him, with pride
He'd planned it well, everything to hand
As through the look-out, the vista, he scanned.

This day was special, for he'd heard
Arrived on the scene, was a very rare bird
With beautiful plumage, the colour of moss
The size of a giant albatross.

He sat quietly waiting, camera in hand
For the Lesser Spotted Hideswiper to land,
After three hours, he was excited to see
There it was, he chuckled with glee!

His patience had paid off, the first to capture
This wonderful sight he viewed in rapture,
But before a good frame he could get into view
It rose into the air, and over him flew.

In seconds, true to its very name
The Hideswiper rendered his hide quite lame,
For in its beak, the hide disappeared
Rising upward, high above him cleared.

The bird-watcher sat perched on his stool
Feeling quite naked, the perfect fool
His hide had been swiped, by this lesser spotted bird
The situation, he knew, was profoundly absurd!

The Looking Glass

The lass looked into a looking glass
There she saw a good looking lass
As she is plain
It's easy to explain
It was her friend looking good in the glass!

The Yobbo on the Bus!

Take a look, there's always one, a yobbo on the bus
He who is obnoxious and really makes a fuss,
Passengers will recognise him, so easy can they spot
A yobbo is unwanted, popular he's not.

My journeys on the bus are eventful every time,
As, over all the empty seats, invariably I climb,
I chew my gum and when I'm done, spit it on the floor
Write graffiti on the windows, and the exit door.

I tap my foot loudly and make a whistling sound
Pick my nose, make a ball, and flick it to the ground,
If anyone complains, my swearing they will hear
And, as I leave the bus, I often hear a cheer.

It's a strategy that works, every single time
On the bus, I act this way, it's not a major crime
This ensures, after such activity and fuss
Next to me, will not sit, the yobbo on the bus!

Three Pound Coins

It was the Young Farmers' Dance at the village hall
When Richard felt the need for nature to call
He went to the Gents and was amazed to spy
Three pound coins in the urinal did lie.

What were they doing lying in there?
For a moment he stood to curiously stare
At the three pound coins, abandoned and soaked
To remove them, for gain, he could not be provoked.

He was disgusted at the very thought
Of putting his hand in, a last resort
He'd have to be desperately short of cash
To retrieve the coins, in his pocket to stash!

Surprising really, when only a few hours before
He'd been assisting a cow, lying in the straw
Putting his hand inside her, to help on its way
The calf she gave birth to that very same day!

It's a Deal!

'Can I borrow your car, Mum?' asked our son, one day.
'If you mow the lawn first, of course you may,'
Was his answer, before we left to go out,
'It's a deal, thanks,' we heard him shout!

But on our return, he caused a fuss
Disgruntled the car keys we'd taken with us,
'Funny,' said his dad, 'we felt sure you'd find
The keys on the mower, we left behind!'

The Cemetery

The cemetery was a perfect burial place
Though, for those living opposite, it seemed not the case,
An argument was fast getting out of hand
They could not be buried in this sacred land.

This was nonsense, the opposition argued
They were getting agitated and very rude,
'Of course they can be buried there,' they said
'No, they can't, for they're not dead!'

Matt's Motor Bike

It was the biggest bike one would ever see
Matt was proud of his constructive ability,
For he'd put it together, all parts were new
A custom-built bike, admiration it drew!

He'd built his motor bike bit by bit
Introducing new parts to the original kit,
Until it was finished, the envy of all
His biking mates, he invited to call.

Truly remarkable, they had to admit
This custom-built monster, from a kit,
But they were to question had he been wise
To construct in his house a bike this size.

'I'm glad you've raised that point,' Matt said,
Of this very moment, he'd been in dread,
'That's why, today, I've invited you all
To get it outside, we've to demolish a wall!'

Window Cleaner Bill

There was a window cleaner called Bill
Who hung by his fingers on a sill
He lost his grip
To the ground did slip
Then rolled to the foot of the hill!

A Clever Pair!

They were such a clever pair, enough to make one sick
As they focused on the future, knew every single trick,
Pets, they had, in plenty, collected all in twos
Dogs and cats and rabbits, and even cockatoos!

Not a normal couple, in fact they were quite odd
Ever looking skyward, in constant touch with God,
Always busy, making plans, which never would they share
A very private couple, who, for no one else did care.

He built a boat, a giant craft, in which to sail away
To take his wife and children off on holiday,
Their pets all went with them, it was an awesome sight
As they departed, in their boat, one very stormy night.

But they could not foresee the rain that came their way
Not so clever, after all, everyone would say,
The rain, it fell in torrents, destined long to pour
Over many weeks, indeed a month, or more.

All thought they'd never see this clever pair again
Lost for ever, kin and pets, in the pouring rain,
But it's well documented, they sailed their way through life
For this very clever pair were Noah and his wife!

His Precious Tool!

His tool was very precious, it was his pride and joy
Its usefulness discovered when he changed to man from
  boy
He cherished it above all other tools he had
He'd the biggest and the best, he was a strapping lad!

To every bed he took it, he'd never be without
Fulfilling expectation, he was never left in doubt,
The ladies, for his services, were always very keen
His energy was tireless, his performance, it was mean.

He used it in the churchyard, in the garden too
By the river, in the park, anywhere would do
Wherever it was needed, no problem did he see
It was there for him to use, his speciality!

It was the tool of his trade, success was guaranteed
Always near to hand, fulfilling every need
He was a landscape gardener, he'd really got it made
With his very precious tool – a trusty garden spade!

Vicki's Hormones

There was a lady called Vicki
Whose hormones were proving tricky
Her treatment went wrong
Being far too strong
Now she's a burly brickie!

Nun Too Happy

The nun left the surgery at considerable speed
As the receptionist noticed she was seething indeed,
She asked the doctor what had previously occurred
For the nun to leave sharply, without a word!

'I told her she was pregnant,' the doctor replied,
'That could never be!' the receptionist cried.
'No,' said the doctor, his face so demure,
'But for the hiccups she had, it was an excellent cure!'

Waiting Up

Waiting up, the worry is very real
After midnight, deep anxiety I feel
You're not home, where are you?
Expected earlier, and long overdue.

With visions of widowhood, in fear I wait
Police on the doorstep, declare you're late
Body identified, funeral plans made
My stomach churning and nerves all frayed.

Your death in the newspaper solemnly reported
Clothes and belongings painfully sorted
Our children comforted, many tears shed
Memories to cherish and hardship ahead.

Then in you come, totally unaware
How worried I've been, waiting there
I've gone through the motions, all but read the will
You, for my heartache, I could cheerfully kill!

The Other Woman

I wanted Bill all to my very own
Not a few snatched hours, always on loan,
For the other, he cared, but we both knew
We belonged together, our love was true.

Bill always made excuses when it got late
Concerned that she'd be laying in wait
Probing with questions he'd rather not face
Trying to avoid his fall from grace.

But I was determined to make him all mine
Soon no longer to tow the line
To leave her he must, to live with me
I knew if he did, so happy we'd be.

The situation must be resolved, for everyone's sake
Now the time had come, the news to break
He'd be leaving her soon, to live with me
His mum's apron ties severed, finally free!

Joker Murray

There was a joker called Murray
Who cooked, for his mates, a curry
It was a great hit
Until he had to admit
He'd used cat food in the curry!

A Dirty Habit

There once was a kitten that spat
It still spat when it grew to a cat
It taught the rabbit
This dirty habit
Then the dog, the hamster and rat!

Trust William!

'I'll wash your car,' offered William, one day
Dad gratefully accepted, without delay
It wasn't often he was as helpful as this,
'He's after something,' cautioned big sis.

'Extra pocket money, is all I ask
I'll do it well and complete the task.'
'Go ahead,' said Dad, with a smile,
'I'll be going out in a little while.'

So William set to, with water and pail
Soap, sponge and hose, he would not fail,
He might be six, but he was a big boy now
To do the job well, he'd show them how!

He was thorough, of that there was no doubt
As when he'd finished, Dad looked out,
Pleased he was with William, for sure
The car was gleaming, he couldn't ask for more.

'Well done, my boy, here's a shiny new pound
In you, I have the best car cleaner around.'
William's face lit up, at his Dad's high praise
Next time, he thought, *I'll ask for a raise!*

Dad then went out in his shiny clean car
But after five minutes, he hadn't gone far,
When the car spluttered and came to a stop
Dad was stranded, caught on the hop!

Back home, William was summoned to him
Dad's face was stern and very grim
'William, it's you I have to thank
For hosing out my petrol tank!'

'But Dad,' cried William, 'I did not know
That cleaning the tank was such a blow
I'm truly sorry for the trouble I've brought.'
No chance of a raise, next time, he thought!

The Axeman and the Worm

There once was a long worm in the grass
Which an axeman chanced to pass
He chopped it in two
To see what it would do
It went this way and that in the grass!

The Snowman

'It's been snowing!' the children shrieked with delight
As they peered through the window at this wonderful sight,
White, crisp snow, as far as they could see
'Let's make a snowman!' they cried with glee.

They rolled the snow, for the body to make
Made the head and sat down for a break.
Puffing and blowing, then came the hardest bit
As they lifted the head on the body to sit.

They were given an old hat from the lady next door
And filled it, for hair, with the rabbit's straw
They placed it then on the snowman's head,
'Now what shall we use for eyes?' they said.

Two pebbles they found were just nicely sized
A long twisted carrot, for the nose, they devised
For the mouth, they were lucky to find half a comb
And the scarf they used was one of their own.

They gave him buttons all down his front
Using knobs of coal, after a lengthy hunt
They took Dad's shoes, to give him feet
Which made their snowman all complete.

All that day, and the next one too
The children played with, you know who.
Including him in their games and play
Snowman, they hoped, was here to stay!

But sadly, of course, that could never be
And when, next morning, they rose to see
Their snowman had melted, all signs of him gone
The children were heartbroken, every one!

Where he'd been, there were some clues
Knobs of coal, Dad's pair of shoes
Pebbles, hat, scarf, half a comb
A carrot, and straw from rabbit's home.

'Never mind,' said Mum, 'he had to go
And Dad's been patient, don't you know,
Barefooted he'll no longer have to be
When his shoes have dried out, after tea!'

The Weatherman

Though the Bank Holiday weather looked set to be warm
The weatherman was forecasting a terrible storm,
The wind would blow with mighty force
Leaving much destruction along its course.

His advice to all was to make secure
Their homes, from the storm, that lay in store,
Take no chances, for it would be wild
Hard to believe with current weather so mild.

People, he said, should not venture out
Should remain at home, avoid the clout
Stay off the roads, where trouble was afoot
With falling trees and power lines cut!

His motive was selfish, to say the least
He'd misled the people, this weatherman beast,
The outlook was perfect, he'd falsely alerted
To ensure on his day trip the roads were deserted!

OAP Status

We're old, we're poor, we're past our prime
We've reached, in life, our twilight time
Over sixty, we hold OAP status now
From work, we took our final bow.

Though hard we worked for many a year
We find it tough, we sadly fear
To manage between each pension day
Now all our savings have seeped away.

Being pensioned off is not much fun
When money's short, with work all done,
Now fully aware that OAP, for sure
Means we're two of many Old And Poor!

Tasty Morsels

The dog, each day, sat outside the butcher's shop
Looking hungry and forlorn, in need of a chop
A bone, a scrap, anything he could get
An old man befriended him – a routine was set.

Each day, the old man, for the dog's benefit would buy
A tasty morsel, the butcher would sigh
Raise his eyebrows, while selling his meat
The dog waited patiently, the next morsel to greet!

Several weeks went by, a regular pattern was set
The man for the dog, tasty morsels would get
The shopkeeper opposite, to the butcher, did say
'It's nice of that man, to feed your dog every day!'

Spotted Minis

They both owned minis of which they were proud
Spotted all over, stood out in a crowd
She favoured small spots, tasteful too
While his were large, in shades of blue!

Spotted minis, like theirs, no one else had
They were pleased and considerably glad
Savouring the novelty of being the only pair
To own spotted minis with customised flair.

They were the talk of the whole neighbourhood
With their spotted minis, together they stood
Both destined to travel so very far
She in her skirt and he in his car!

Do or Die!

His rope was broken, it was useless now
To scale this cliff, he wondered how,
It was do or die, this time, he knew
The fear within him grew, and grew.

There was a lake below him, a waterfall to the right
The cliff was steep with barely a crevice in sight,
In danger he was from foaming waters below
He hung on tight, his spirits were low.

The water beneath him was rising fast
His pace he quickened, hoping it could last
Wishing he had taken a different path
Not that of a spider in the bath!

The Traffic Warden

Alun returned to his car where a traffic warden stood
With pen poised ready, he'd try if he could
To persuade the warden not to book him this time
Use flattery and compliments to deflect his crime.

The warden responded to his easy patter
Alun thought he was clever to clear this matter,
She would, this once, turn a blind eye, she said
As she smiled sweetly, and looked straight ahead.

She left him then, as he breathed a sigh
Relieved that the warden had passed him by
He got in his car, turned the ignition on
Pleased with himself, he'd soon be gone.

But his car would not move off the yellow lines
Where before he'd parked and escaped many fines,
When he alighted the car, his foot he angrily stamped
As he realised, all along, his car had been clamped!

Eight Months Pregnant!

After the first ever row with her hubby she flew
Out of the house, as her emotions grew,
Eight months pregnant, holding back a tear
Just a temporary upset but her distress was clear.

Her eyes were filling, as she neared the church
Past weeping willows and silver birch,
Her hanky, she held, close to her tearful face
As she joined a funeral, just taking place.

Naturally now, her tears could freely flow
The real reason, no one would ever know,
She'd stand at the back, unobtrusive and still
But, two ladies eyed her, with looks that could kill.

Though they spoke quietly, she heard one say to the other
'I knew he was a rogue, my elder brother
Look, she's expecting, it's plain to see!'
Her companion replied, 'But he was eighty-three!'

My Dream Home!

It had taken years of work and honest toil
Planning my dream home – fit for a royal
Gradually introducing the furniture I rated
And weeding out that which I'd always hated.

Systematically each room had been carefully planned
For the right curtains and carpets, every shop scanned,
Pictures and ornaments chosen with decor in mind
All colour co-ordinated, with beauty combined.

The finishing touch was to be the suite
The day had come, my dream home was complete,
In less than an hour, after long years awaited
At last, all my desires were finally sated.

The delivery men arrived with the suite on time
I opened the door and heard myself chime,
'I've waited ten years for this,' and was blasted then,
'The fault's not ours, we're just delivery men!'

Please Don't Wake Me Yet

Please don't wake me yet, my dream is not quite through
You see, I'm with our loved ones, in a world so new,
A heavenly place where angels herald them in rows
Where everything is perfect and time just never goes.

I see my dear old Dad, without his walking stick
His sister, Nan, walks tall and straight, and is no longer
    sick,
Gran is now sprightly, before I never saw her so
Brother Rich, so handsome, why did he have to go?

I see my Auntie Isabel and Mary's here as well
And beautiful Auntie Beryl, she really is a belle,
Please don't wake me yet, it's too good to be true
I see Mary and Roland, Grandma and Grandad too!

Please don't wake me yet, I've missed them all so much
I want to stay a while, find a way to keep in touch,
But it's too late, you've roused me, now they have gone for
    sure
Our loved ones have departed back through Heaven's door!

Our Love Affair

Our love affair is over, it had to end some day
You always left me breathless, there was no other way,
Though I loved you dearly, and miss you avidly
Common sense prevailed, the end just had to be.

Don't think I will forget you, I never ever will
My love for you was true, you're in my system still,
Addicted by your presence, though I knew it was a sin
I wanted you, I didn't care, but I could never win.

Occasionally, I see you, out with someone new
That's when I miss you most, now that we are through,
My heart beats a little faster, but I shouldn't have regrets
Because I'm so much better since I gave up cigarettes!

A Perfect Pair

They're a pair, they should always be together
Inside and out, whatever the weather
Made for each other, a quality rare
An enduring twosome, a perfect pair.

They're always so close, within a stride
Complementing each other, side by side
Their warmth is constant, together they share
The recognition of being a perfect pair.

But I'm left to wonder, when a wash is completed,
Why a perfect pair is suddenly depleted
Leaving me short of adequate stocks
My clothes basket full of many odd socks!

Paul's Tooth

It came out with a toffee, though he wasn't aware
Until the gap in his mouth, he discovered there,
Swallowed with the toffee, the tooth had departed
Six-year-old Paul was very downhearted.

It had been the first tooth he'd had come out
The one, for days, he'd wiggled about,
Making his tongue sore, as it explored
This tooth, at Paul, that niggled and gnawed.

Now the tooth was gone, his concern was great
What action must be taken? What would be his fate?
It was needed to leave for the tooth fairy to collect
In exchange for a coin – his plan was wrecked.

Surgery was not needed, his mother assured Paul
He would have to wait for nature to call,
In the fullness of time, the fairy could collect
The tooth that his body would surely reject!

Candid Camera

Of his new camera, Joe was very proud
He would make a living, he'd often vowed,
He studied a book, to glean all he should know
It looked so easy, he'd soon be a pro.

He loaded it up with film and flash
Batteries too, then had a bash,
Through the view finder he would stare
Until his chosen frame was there.

Joe pressed the button, the picture taken
Then moved to the next, the first forsaken,
Again he focused and pressed away
The perfect shot before him lay.

He took pictures indoors, outdoors too
Animals, people, no matter who,
Flora, fauna, anything that moved
His camera genius would soon be proved.

The film all finished, away it was sent
As soon as possible, for development,
The result of his efforts, he was anxious to see
How good his photos would turn out to be.

When the prints were returned to him
Some were bright, some were dim,
Under-exposed, or the focus out
All were bad, without a doubt.

Joe's disappointment was clear to see
He knew a photographer he'd never be,
He'd hoped this way his living to earn
But it seemed he still had much to learn!

A Hard Lesson!

The teacher was never in control of her class
The kids had no hope of their exams to pass
For they would not settle in lessons to learn
And she was unable, their respect to earn.

Every lesson, kids would be sent to the Head
The weak, by the strong, were fearlessly led,
Misbehaviour was rife, Mrs Maine had no chance
When trying to maintain an authoritative stance.

The kids, one day, before Mrs Maine arrived
A dastardly trick had devilishly contrived,
A live match, in her chalk, was carefully encased
Then, next to the blackboard, strategically placed.

Mrs Maine greeted her class, on that day
Amazed at the attention they appeared to pay,
This was not the Class 4B she knew and hated
Could this be the day she'd long awaited?

The kids held their breath when she took the chalk
As it scratched the board, she let out a squawk,
The match had ignited with the desired effect
Mrs Maine's nerves were shattered and totally wrecked.

She screamed as she ran from the class of 4B
As the kids all laughed with absolute glee,
She ran from the school and down the lane
Like someone demented and quite insane!

The kids of 4B were to regret that day
For Mrs Maine's class went to Mr Kray,
He was tough, strict and extremely stern
A hard lesson, indeed, 4B had to learn!

Postcard Home

Dear Mavis, having a good time in Spain
I helped the pilot fly the plane!
The hotel is ideal, the food is great
I've found myself a steady date!

The weather here is sunny too
My room has a splendid view
There's plenty to do and lots to see,
It really is the place to be!

I've seen flamenco dancers, bullfighters too
Done all the things that tourists do
I've been swimming in the deep blue sea
And fallen asleep beneath a tree!

I love it here, I'd like to stay
But know you miss me, when I'm away.
Don't worry, I'll soon be coming home
All my love – your garden gnome!

Marriage Upset

The marriage was rocky, she'd known for a while
Their differences she'd tried hard to reconcile,
But she was now sure there was someone else in his life
That he no longer needed her as his wife!

The love they'd shared was all diminished
It was a matter of time before they were finished
Bitter she was for she knew she still cared
Most reluctant to give up the life they shared.

Of course, he denied there was someone new
But telltale signs gave her a different view,
He'd arrive home hours after he was due
His movements unexplained, no plausible clue!

Determined the truth to establish at last
She set out to follow him, the die was cast,
For she was to discover his secret that day
He was meeting a man, her husband was gay!

Stock Still

He was standing stock still, no movement she saw
He must be cold, the wind was raw,
Though he wore a coat, it was open wide
He clutched a stick, his legs were astride.

What he was doing, Tracey could not tell
Though a distance away, her eyes befell
A peaked hat he wore, against the cold
She'd often seen him, a sight to behold.

This day, she thought she could no longer defer
Her curiosity had got the better of her,
It was quite a walk, she leapt a stile
And crossed a field, some half a mile.

Standing stock still, he was quite unaware
Tracey was getting closer, nearly there,
Until right beside him, she was to stand
So close, she could touch the scarecrow's hand!

The Crunch

Sometimes, in the office, hunger can persist
An apple, on the desk, then is hard to resist,
No one will know, you can take a bite
Stave off your hunger, out of sight!

You take that bite, a mouthful indeed
Penetrating through to the core, and the seed,
As you munch away, the phone then rings
What a dilemma this inevitably brings.

Two choices you have, which will it be?
Let it ring, until you're free,
Your mouth is clear, of apple bereft
By then, your caller's probably left!

Or spit it out, to take the call
An action taking no time at all,
But when finished, you're still hungry no doubt
And obliged to find the piece you spat out!

Embarrassing Teenagers!

Lynn was embarrassed, being seen out with us
Her beloved parents, for she made a big fuss,
When calling her name in a public place
She took exception to this, fearing loss of face.

We decided next time Lynn's attention was needed
In a public place, tact should be heeded,
We'd call out 'Sophie', then she would know
We wanted to leave, it was a signal to go!

The next time a situation like this occurred
It was her brother who needed a tactful word,
He knew the arrangement, we hoped he'd comprehend
As I shouted 'Sophie', the message to send!

Immediately, he responded 'Just one more minute, Mum!'
With odd looks returned, we went white and numb,
Left to wonder of our two teenage children then
If *we* really wanted to be seen out with *them*!

You!

You provide us with the warmth we crave
With energy, our time you save
You wash, you cook and clean for us
Always there, without a fuss.

You generate music, we love to hear
Entertain us all, throughout the year,
You press our clothes and wash the dishes
Without complaint, you fulfil our wishes.

The light you radiate helps us to see
How privileged we must always be,
To have you there, at beck and call
Taken for granted by one and all.

But this all changes when you go away
Causing chaos at home, even just for a day,
Your true value, Electricity, cannot be ignored
While we await your power to be restored!

Birthday Surprise

Nicky told no one what she was planning to do
As, from the airport lounge, she withdrew,
She was flying from Australia to her hometown of Rhyl
To give her mother a surprise birthday thrill.

Though living far apart they always kept in touch
Were very close, missed each other so much,
They talked regularly on the telephone
Clocking up hours, if the truth be known.

Her mother was alone, since her father departed
Nicky knew, on this day, she'd be downhearted,
She decided there was only one thing to do
So she bought a ticket and home she flew.

Nicky was so excited she could hardly wait
As she reached her mother's house, opened the gate,
Knocked on the door, a bouquet in her hand
The door remained closed, there she was left to stand.

Her mother's neighbour looked out from next door
Nicky was to stare, drop the flowers to the floor
As the neighbour explained her mother was far away
Flown to Australia, to surprise Nicky, that day!

Milkmaid Mary

There was a milkmaid called Mary
Who went to work in a dairy
But she dyed the milk red
White was boring, she said
Now she no longer works at the dairy!

The Pig

There once was a lively fat pig
Who, at breakfast was dancing a jig
At lunch, the samba
At tea, the rumba
By supper, he was a tired thin pig!

Santa is Dead!

The tears were falling down Emily's cheek
She was sobbing so much she couldn't speak,
Her mother was alarmed, 'Whatever's wrong?'
But Emily just cried, hard and long.

After a while, she calmed enough to say
'There'll be no presents on Christmas Day
I've seen the notice, Santa is dead
I can't believe what I've just read.'

As her mother looked on, Emily continued to cry,
'I'm only six, but I want to die!
Christmas won't be the same, if Santa can't come
The thought of it all just makes me numb!'

In her mother's arms, her tears eventually ceased
Emily was despondent, to say the least,
Her mother said, 'I'm sure Santa is alive and well.'
Emily said, 'I'll show you, it's the truth I tell!'

She led her mother to the notice and said,
'Look, here it says, "Santa is ded".'
'No,' laughed her mother, 'It's ripped, the rest is there,
Santa is ded… icated to children everywhere!'

The Christmas Dinner

Christmas was coming, a week to go
Turkey was forlorn, head held low,
The farmyard animals were in sympathy too
As they'd heard what next the farmer must do.

The chickens, pigs, sheep and goats
All had big lumps in their throats
At the thought of Turkey as Christmas dinner
She was the prize, but not the winner.

It was only Goose who strutted and cavorted
Who cared not of the rumours reported
Pleased she'd be to see Turkey perish
Her place she'd take and always cherish!

All the animals loved Turkey the best
While Goose was pushed out of the farmyard nest
Bossy she was – they took exception to this
And always ill-tempered, with a nasty hiss.

Meanwhile, the farmer was preparing to act
For it was a cruel Christmas fact
That Turkey should grace the festive meal
Now he was ready, her fate to seal!

The necessary deed was quickly done
He then broke the news to his wife and son
'I fancy a change, I have to say
We're having Goose on Christmas Day!'

The Pantoland Ball

It was Pantoland's event of the year
All the characters would soon appear
Jack, without the Giant, would come
Cinderella, Aladdin and Tom Thumb.

Peter Pan was coming too
Captain Hook and all his crew
Dick Whittington with Babes in the Wood
Simple Simon and Robin Hood.

The Dwarfs were coming with Snow White
The Good Fairy's wand would be shining bright
Alice in Wonderland and the White Rabbit too
Would all be attending this glittering do.

Even Scrooge was expected to attend
The Wizard of Oz would bring a friend
Sleeping Beauty would be wide awake
The Panto Dame had baked a cake.

The Prince arrived on the Panto Horse
The Princess was the prettiest, of course
As the evening wore on, the characters agreed
The Pantoland Ball was the finest indeed.

Then it was time for the Prince to declare
His love for the beautiful Princess, fair
He kissed her lips, her eyes were agog
As the handsome Prince turned into a frog!

One's Inconvenience

This story isn't funny, you mustn't laugh
It really caused One pain and a half,
It happened while shopping, One felt the need
For a public convenience, and quickly indeed.

One's tummy was upset, One had to make haste
As on the seat One's self urgently placed,
One did One's business, feeling better for that
Then One was to feel one hell of a prat!

One could not rise, One was firmly stuck
Though each and every effort One took,
Someone was guilty, One knew not who
Of covering the seat with superglue!

One was flustered in embarrassing state
All One could do was sit and wait
For someone to come, the alarm to raise
Hospital treatment would be One's next phase!

From this inconvenience, One was eventually extracted
At the hospital, One's attention was suddenly attracted,
Immediately, One knew the evil culprit was found
His fingers, with superglue, were bonded and bound!

Dog-Lover Pat

There was a dog-lover called Pat
Whose dog was fast losing fat
It wasn't the fact
A diet was cracked
More that he was chasing the cat!

Upside-Down Pete

There was a young man called Pete
Who hung upside-down by his feet
The blood rushed to his head
Turning his face quite red
Though white as a sheet were his feet!

The Lady on the Bus

The lady was causing a bit of a fuss
As she sat, in her seat, at the front of the bus,
The youth beside her was quietly reading a book
As she cast on him a disdainful look.

A respectable youth, with hair neat and trim
His appearance was smart, but the lady was grim,
She nudged him on purpose, made tutting sounds
Though her actions were unfair, on moral grounds.

He could not understand what he'd done to upset
This lady who he'd never before met,
He decided it was best, that he should ignore
The rudeness of the lady next door.

Suddenly, she viciously stamped on his toe
He stared at the lady, an unlikely foe,
He vacated his seat without a word
This lady's behaviour was quite absurd.

He moved to a seat further down the bus
Soon to realise why she'd caused such a fuss,
The lady was beckoning plainly, you see
To her friend, to sit in the seat he'd made free!

Bad News

The policeman was nervous, he'd not done it before
As he plucked up courage to knock on the door,
He'd some very bad news he had to impart
What would he say? How would he start?

The door was opened by a middle-aged man
He took a deep breath, then he began,
'I'm sorry, it's bad news, can I come in?'
As he stepped over the threshold, to gain entry within.

The man beckoned him through to the sitting room
Fearing the worst, his face full of gloom,
'You've come to tell me someone's died
Don't say it's my wife,' he sorrowfully cried.

The policeman took a sharp intake of breath
Before imparting news of the victim's death,
'I've come to tell you that Abe Smith's passed away
Died of a heart attack earlier today!'

The man's reaction was not as he'd expected
For his face lit up, he was far from dejected,
'You've made a mistake, officer, it's plain to see
The dead man's not Abe Smith, for I am he!'

Make, Mend and Bust It

Joiners called Make, Mend and Bust It
Over a table, had generally fussed it
Solid was the top
But the legs were a flop
As they dropped to the floor, they cussed it!

The Nude Model

There was a nude model called Ray
Who was posing in art class one day
Though much he was baring
He insisted on wearing
His socks, on the couch, where he lay!

Sweet Reserve

It was a beautiful, appealing, luxury box
Of wonderful, exquisite, tasty chocs
Bought abroad with currency strange
Appearing cheap, though top of the range.

It was only after the purchase was made
Karen realised the extent of her unwise trade
She never would have bought them, had she known
They were treble the price she'd have paid at home.

However, the best she would make of the deal
She'd keep them, for they had special appeal,
Until such time a suitable occasion arose
With them she could impress, and even pose.

That event occurred some few months later
In luxurious surroundings, her chocolates would cater
Adding to the grandeur of the occasion they deserved
She'd open this box of confectionery reserved.

To share her treasure, the time was now right
Her box of chocolates, Karen displayed with delight,
Then she became agitated, in embarrassed state
Suddenly aware, they were weeks out of date!

The Ice Skater

There was a young ice-skater called Price
Who circled on one spot on the ice
One minute he was there
Next, the rink was bare
As he'd cut through a hole in the ice!

A Fishy Tale!

The fishing competition was an annual event
When all entrants would aim with intent
To catch the highest weight in fish
And claim the prestigious winner's dish.

This day, Richard was convinced he could win
Last year, he'd lost by a tail and a fin,
So he cast his line and sat in wait
For the fish to rise to his tasty bait.

He caught one fish, but of no weight to boast
Doing his best, catching more than most,
But soon he was to fall well behind of the rest
As his opponents caught some of the very best.

He was beginning to think his luck was out
It got even worse, without a doubt,
His opponents all turned to laugh and hoot
When out of the water he pulled an old boot.

But the last laugh Richard was about to enjoy
This boot would frustrate and certainly annoy,
His opponents, to him, had lost the match
For a fish, in the boot, proved the heaviest catch!

Football Crazy

The game was crucial, with a trophy at stake
They had to win, the glory to take
3–2 down, was the half-time score
Their supporters willed them to go for more.

In the second half, their confidence grew
Fletcher scored a goal and level they drew
Then a penalty was scored by the opposition
4–3 then was the nail-biting position.

Beaty volleyed off the post, to level the score
Making it a most respectable 4–4
Five minutes to go, they were desperate to get
One more ball in the back of the net.

Russell came from nowhere, and took the ball
The crowd went wild, a goal to enthral
As it passed the goalkeeper, he looked upset
A fifth goal scored, the ball in the net.

The referee blew his whistle in haste
The last three minutes he would not waste
But Jack Russell's goal he would not allow
The terrier must leave the pitch right now!

The Dirty Old Chap

Albert Brown was a dirty old chap
Who coaxed the lasses to sit on his lap
Until Melanie Clark
Left a very wet mark
Which cured the dirty old chap!

Clock Chaos

I'd put my clocks forward, before going to bed
So had to rise earlier to stay ahead
I was visiting a friend and had to strive
On time, on the hour of noon to arrive.

Claire was surprised to see me then
'The clocks went back, it's only ten!'
She protested my timing was two hours out
But I was soon to convince her, allay any doubt.

So forward by two hours she moved her clock
Everything went fine, after her initial shock
Lunch, though late, was a most enjoyable affair
As we giggled at the error, made by Claire.

It was nearly four when I had to depart
Thanked Claire for lunch, a work of art!
While driving home, the radio, my attention it drew
When a voice announced the News at Two.

Dare I tell Claire she was right all along
The clocks went back, that I was wrong?
I knew I'd have to explain very soon
Why we'd gained two hours that afternoon!

Kids of Today

The kids of today are wired for sound
Music to their ears, as they play around
Sticking in lugs
Like shiny black bugs
Making them deaf to the world around!

The Ship's Cook

There was a ship's cook who was hired
Concerned that his captain looked tired
'The seagulls kept me awake,'
Complained Captain Blake,
'Don't serve them again, or you're fired!'

Jumble Gesture

The Scouts were organising a jumble sale
Marion was pleased, for it would entail
Her having a sort-out of unwanted gear
She'd accumulated a lot, it was very clear.

She discarded the clothes she didn't wear
Things for which she no longer did care
Dresses hardly worn and nearly new
Skirts and blouses, to name but a few.

The awful handbag she'd hidden away
Came out of the cupboard where it lay
Brand new, though for it no love was lost
As on to the pile it was carelessly tossed.

All this unwanted gear she bagged and sent
To the sale, where her Scout sons went
They helped sell the jumble, the funds to swell
And even bought some things as well.

They returned home with games, books and toys
The sort of things that appeal to boys
They'd also bought Marion a special gift
The awful handbag, she'd cast adrift!

Her Husband

Her husband was dressed in a dress
She was shocked, and nothing less
'You can't go out
Without a doubt
With no tights on, you look a mess!'

A Girl Among Boys!

I'm the only girl in a big family of boys
Expected to be quiet, while they make a noise,
To keep the place tidy, while they make a mess
Scruffy jeans they can wear, for me it's a dress.

The unfairness of being a girl among boys
They have more fun, and such exciting toys,
For me it's a doll, they have robots and cars
I have a skipping rope, they fly to Mars!

While out playing, all is equal for a while
Until caught short, in their inimitable style
The wall then is refuge for their relief,
If I even considered it, I'd come to grief!

If they misbehave, it's ignored every time
But if I were to err, it's a punishable crime,
Not the behaviour, I'm told, of a young lady with poise
They are exempt because 'boys will be boys'!

But there's one consolation being a girl among boys
I'm a quiet young lady, with manners and poise,
Tidy in my outlook, always beautifully dressed
People tut at the boys, with me they're impressed!

Chocolates Galore

It was a giant tin of chocolate sweets
Full of delicious wrapped-up treats,
Noisette whirls and Orange cremes
Fulfilling all my sweetest dreams.

Coffee creams and toffees galore
Walnut whirls, I wanted more,
Soft fruity centres, a Turkish delight
A chocolate miniature, heavenly bite.

Toffee fingers, so sweet and chewy
Strawberry roses, nice and gooey,
Fudge and hazelnuts in caramel
They all went down so very well!

Pralines next, I had to eat
Plain chocolate too, a delightful treat,
Montelimar and brazil nuts went
And nutty truffle, heaven sent!

The tin is empty, where did they go?
Those wonderful chocolates, that I love so,
Delicious confectionery, creamy and thick
Now, for my sin, I'm feeling sick!

The Job Seeker

There was a job seeker called France
Who thought she was in with a chance
Until she left the room
Then was filled with gloom
For her skirt was tucked in her pants!

Two Inches Over!

On business, Malcolm was flying abroad
He would need a bag he could carry on board,
To keep with him, and so travel light
He was only away for one single night.

He'd only one bag, it would have to do
He checked his ticket to give him a clue,
If it fell within the rules of the Airline
Two inches over – surely that would be fine!

As he walked to the plane, ticket in hand
An official approached, his bag was banned,
Too big for hand luggage, he was told
It was taken away, to be stored in the hold.

Having completed all business at his flight destination
The size of his bag caused him much fascination,
For it must have shrunk, as his bag was allowed
On the homeward flight, with the passenger crowd.

The moral of this story is easy to guess
Being two inches over, can cause distress,
When flying out, you'll certainly get caught
But when flying back, two inches is naught!

A Man Called West

There was a man called West
Who was destroying a magpie's nest
The magpie was perturbed
At being disturbed
And promptly crapped on his chest!

The Cock

The cock constantly crowed before dawn
Woke the neighbours every morn
They were all very cross
So it was no loss
When the cock was found dead on the lawn!

Ann's Puncture

Ann was alone when the puncture occurred
In twenty years driving, it was quite absurd,
It had never happened in her life before
She'd need help with this, of that she was sure.

She held no membership of services to assist
She'd let it lapse, when renewal she'd missed,
Where the wheel changing tools were, she had no clue
How to drive the vehicle was all she knew.

Ann decided to stand, a picture of feminine helplessness
Hoping a caring male driver would spot her distress
Offer to help, and put things right,
The next moment one was to come into sight.

A motorcyclist stopped, having seen her plight
He sat for a moment then moved to alight,
He looked at the puncture, he looked at Ann
Then returned to his bike, and menacingly began:

'I cannot believe, in this age, when equality is rife
That to a lady a wheel change causes such strife!'
With that he laughed, and with no backward glance
Left Ann, aghast, open-mouthed in her stance!

Wonder Watch

Harvey showed off his new watch with pride
Its durability could not be denied,
To demonstrate its full hardiness
Some tricks he performed, his mates to impress.

First he threw his watch against the wall
Cast it as hard as a cricket ball,
Then he immersed it full in his beer
As it sank to the bottom, his mates gave a cheer.

Now this watch of his was a mighty fine piece
In telling the time it would never cease,
For all the roughness it had to endure
He knew in his watch, there was no flaw!

Of course, all his mates had to agree
Indestructible his watch must surely be
To withstand the rough treatment they had seen,
He'd purposely been so hard and mean!

Next time they met, Harvey's wrist was bare
'No watch today? Surely not in for repair?'
'Of course not,' he said, 'just a slight mishap,
The watch is fine, I've broken the strap!'

Undertaker Pat

There was an undertaker called Pat
Who, at a funeral, lost his hat
His head was bared
The mourners stared
As his wig came off with his hat!

Snail Tale!

Little Jimmy was helping his dad, in the garden, one day
When their neighbour looked over the fence, to say
How much the snails were causing him concern
Ruining each of his prize vegetables, in turn!

Jimmy's dad sympathised, confirming he'd also had a few
But no damage they'd had a chance to do
Jimmy said, 'Do what my dad does' – his dad went tense
As Jimmy advised, 'Toss them over the fence!'

The Auction

Dawn sat at the auction on the right-hand side
A beautiful piece of china, she'd spied,
Determined to have it, at any price
The auctioneer's eye she'd catch and entice!

The bidding had started, she tried her best
The piece to buy, to seriously invest,
But the auctioneer didn't look her way
Not once towards her his eyes did stray.

Was the man blind, couldn't he see?
Dawn wanted this china desperately
So sure she was, if she stood on a chair
He'd finally catch sight of her bidding there.

As the hammer went down, her footing she lost
Though the china wasn't hers, it dearly cost,
For, at the auction, a broken arm she got
And left with a plaster of Paris pot!

Book Bound!

He was a bookworm, of the highest order
A constant reader, a regular hoarder,
Over many years, he'd accumulated a stack
Read each book once, then kept them back.

The cellar was full, his wife would despair
For he'd never know, if they weren't there,
She took that chance, one day, when she saw
An ad for old books, in the local store.

Several weeks later, when the cellar was bare
He announced his intention to attend a book fair,
His wife was on edge as he left that night
Knowing most books there were his by right.

On his return, she was relieved to see
He was empty-handed, she smiled with glee,
He explained there were no new books to enthral
For he was lucky enough to have them all!

The Cuckoo!

'Cuckoo! Cuckoo!' it's a beautiful sound
Take the time to listen, if you are around,
She's not that popular with other birds
But we all appreciate her timely words.

She's the one on whom we can rely
When we hear her song, above us high,
It's the spring that sets her on her way
To sing to us throughout the day.

She has an hourly ritual that never stops
Out from her nest she regularly pops,
Constantly aware of the sound of 'tick tock'
For she is the cuckoo in the clock!

Motorbike Mad!

Ben was little, and motorbike mad
Every time he saw one, he shrieked at his dad,
'Look at that, oh isn't it great
One day I'll have one, I just can't wait!'

His dad always said to his son of five,
'Never, as long as I am alive,'
He hated motorbikes and the thought of his son
Endangering his life, only just begun.

One day, Ben was talking to his friend
When a motorbike zoomed round the bend,
Excitedly, he exclaimed, to his friend's surprise
'I'm having one of them, when my father dies!'

Pills

Pills, you try to tempt me, urging me to take
An overdose to oblivion, from which I'd never wake,
Life is full of upset, no longer can I cope
What's the point of living, when I only want to mope?

Jilted by my boyfriend, whom I thought was ever true
Until he told me it was over, our relationship was through,
I cannot live without him, nor do I want to try
Should I take you, Pills, and lie down here to die?

No, Pills, you're not the answer – I have to face the pain
The hurt and dented ego and learn to live again,
He wasn't all that perfect, clear I now can see
Blinded by my love was I, he's not the man for me.

At sixteen, I should not despair, there are better men than
     him
My first lost love now fading, no need to be so grim!
I'll find in time my true love, some day he'll come along
So, Pills, you cannot tempt me, my zest for life is strong!

Road Rage

Two ladies met down a narrow country lane
Bumper to bumper in the pouring rain
Their cars not able to proceed anywhere fast
One irate lady, on her horn, gave a blast!

The second dithered, not knowing what to do
She'd wait to see if the other withdrew
But the lady stood fast, for it was her right of way
Expecting the other's reversal to the passing bay!

So this is how the two ladies stayed
Until another driver, an appearance made
He drew up behind the lady who was irate
Due at a meeting, now he'd likely be late!

He approached the ditherer, his face was bitter
He felt so cross, he could have hit her
Then he became aware of the lady's distress
His anger subsided, he'd sort out this mess!

'I'm sorry,' she cried, 'I don't know what to do
I feel such an idiot, for I don't have a clue
It's my husband's car, before I've never been near
Perhaps you can point out the reversing gear!'

Dyslexic Jake

There was a dyslexic icer called Jake
Who had decorated a birthday cake
Though it looked superb
The teenager was perturbed
As Jake had iced '81' on the cake!

Ivor, the Ski Boat Driver

There was a ski boat driver called Ivor
Who had ambitions beyond a driver
He hit a big rock
And got a cold shock
As he became a ski boat diver!

Shopper Stopper

The pair were chatting for five minutes or more
They'd met in the local grocery store,
Doing their shopping, it was quite by chance
As Natalie stared at the shelves, in a trance.

Deliberating, she was, whether to have one or two
Of the special offer she saw on view,
When this lady appeared, with her grown-up son
Greeted her warmly, their conversation begun!

How was she? It had been a long time!
Is the family well? Hers was fine!
They were preparing to holiday, had she been yet?
They'd been to Barbados since last they met!

She rabbited on, her son stood quietly to one side
Not even attempting, his boredom to hide,
At last their chat was over, all news imparted
They exchanged good wishes, and both departed.

Natalie stared as she looked after the pair
She'd not let on, but she was well aware
The lady thought Natalie was someone she knew,
And, who *she* was, Natalie hadn't a clue!

The Lady from Bowlyn

There was a lady from Bowlyn
Who had a bag with coal in
But a trail she left
And was rendered bereft
As her bag had a dirty big hole in!

Wind and Moon

Wind looked across the sky at night
And there he saw Moon shining bright,
Her brightness dazzled, he was fierce and grim
He would blow and blow until Moon was dim.

So blow he did and Moon went away
Glad was Wind to keep her at bay,
For he was stronger, no contest there
To return again Moon would not dare.

Wind was surprised when Moon reappeared
The bright shining orb nonchalantly leered,
Wind was angry and blew as hard as he could
Though Moon for a while, her ground, she stood!

Soon Wind was victorious, as Moon diminished
That's it, he thought now she's finished,
I've shown Moon who is infinite boss
And her dazzling brightness will be no loss.

Of course, the next night Moon would be there
For, of Wind, she was totally unaware
As, high in the sky, she would forever shine,
Wind just an element, Moon divine!

He Snores!

He snores when together we spend the night
With loud, rhythmic, resounding might,
Keeps me awake for hours on end
Drives me up and round the bend.

Should I, to the spare room, take myself off
Give him a sharp nudge, emit a cough,
Prod him and poke him, give him a shake
Until he stops snoring, or he's wide awake.

It's a dangerous condition that could probably kill
Me, him, when I've had my fill!
It's a kind of torture, it drives me mad
When morning comes, I'm always glad!

He wakes up refreshed, when I'm done in
His snoring really is a mortal sin,
All day I yawn, so tired I feel
I really am getting a very poor deal.

Though I love him, it's a tiresome thing
His snoring, for me, no peace will it bring,
I know he can't help it, he's not to blame
I wonder, does his wife feel the same!

Harry Malone

There was a man called Harry Malone
Who didn't like sleeping on his own
So he forced the cat
On the bed from the mat
But the cat preferred sleeping alone!

Shoed Off!

The neighbour's dog was causing a racket
Ian was in bed, he couldn't hack it,
It was early, he'd planned to sleep awhile
But the yapping was constant, guaranteed to rile.

No more could he take, to the window he leapt
Opened it wide, aside curtains he swept,
He grabbed his shoe and aimed his best
Tossing it hard at the canine pest.

The trespassing dog in his garden below
Recognised it was time to turn and go,
The yapping had ceased, but Ian's relief was brief
As it scarpered with his shoe – the canine thief!

Jenny's Wobbly Jelly!

Jenny's wobbly jelly, would not come out
In the mould, it was stuck, without a doubt,
Until she remembered a tip, previously heard
She crossed to the sink, as the thought occurred!

The mould Jenny held under a very hot tap
To free the jelly and ease her flap,
But one thing she'd forgotten, she did not think
Detached at last, it plopped into the sink!

Doctor Short

Jamie's visit to the doctor was a serious affair
That he was ill, he was very aware,
He waited a while, until his name was called
Summoned to the surgery, and duly installed.

The doctor must be one of the locums, he thought
For he was not the regular, Doctor Short,
As Jamie started to speak, the doctor looked intent
Listening most carefully, with head slightly bent.

Jamie related his symptoms, and he could confirm
They were getting worse, and causing concern,
He hoped the doctor could diagnose and treat
The illness he was most anxious to beat.

As he spoke, Jamie was thinking he'd seen the doctor
    before
Though, not at the surgery, he was sure,
Perhaps at the hospital, when he'd last been there
He just could not remember exactly where.

The doctor then rose, he was wearing one sock
His other foot was bare, it was quite a shock,
For he then admitted he was a patient too
Doctor Short had popped out to the loo!

Now Jamie remembered where he'd seen him before
He knew he'd been caught out, this time for sure,
His life insurance man's wrath, he could not avoid
Who'd only grant cover, if good health was enjoyed!

Teenage Torment

Seeing your face is all I need
A few kind words, a gesture in deed,
To see your smile, to catch your eye
Why do I love you enough to die?

You're under my skin, I can't think straight
How to get through this day, I must contemplate,
If I do not see you, the day is so long
Why do I love you with this heart so strong?

I long to be so secure in your arms
You would hold me tight, I'd bask in your charms,
You'd declare your love and we'd never part
Why do I love you with all my heart?

My love is one-sided, I must declare
I do not exist, you are unaware,
How my heart pounds when you're close to me
Why do I love you so desperately?

Your kindness is your nature and nothing more
I'm not special, just one of a score,
You're a popular person, at your feet ladies fall
Why do I love you when you care not at all?

It's a teenage torment, this love of mine
My teacher, you are, please give me a sign.
I'm told it's not right, it's even bad
Why do I love you – you're as old as my dad!

The Old Days!

Her grandson listened intently, of old days long gone by
To understand how life was then she wanted him to try,
He'd seen the old movies and felt Granny's life was dull
Without today's inventions that made his life so full.

'Granny,' he said, 'I'm so very glad we live now as we do
With everything in colour, bright and clear and true,
Before colour was invented when you lived in black and
    white
The old days weren't so brilliant, with only dark and light!'

The Beggar!

He sits huddled in a doorway, as people pass him by
His clothes are very tatty, his cloth cap lies nearby
Inviting coins from shoppers, with pity in their eyes,
Such a sorry sight, for help his countenance cries.

With the white cane by his side, he makes a rhythmic tap
As members of the public generously fill his cap,
Their concern is very evident, a poor blind man they see
All too pleased to spare a coin, to show their sympathy!

When the day is over and all the shoppers leave
He shuffles to his feet, stuffs his takings up his sleeve,
He slowly makes his exit, until he's sure no one can see
Then the beggar drops his cane and drives home for his tea!

Free Mum!

'Go get help!' she cried out, in obvious distress
The children had to free Mum from this embarrassing
　　mess,
To the phone box they hastened, 999 to ring,
'Come quickly,' they pleaded, 'Mum needs rescuing!'

To the park, the fire brigade rushed, on the children's
　　appeal
Their mother was in shock at her terrible ordeal,
The professionals arrived, their rescue experience to bring
Mum's bum was stuck tight in the park's children's swing!

Job Dissatisfaction

'I'm going to tell my boss just what I think,'
Said Johnny, to his mate, over a midnight drink,
'What's more, I'll put it in writing now,'
Stevie looked at him, with furrowed brow!

'Do you think it's a good idea,
Wait until your mind is clear
Do nothing hasty, that you will regret,'
But he wouldn't listen, his mind was set!

Johnny took out a pen, and started to write
Listing his grievances, with all his might,
Stevie looked on, not believing he dare
Put in writing, what he thought was unfair!

'He'll never take this, you'll lose your place
At the factory, the sack you'll surely face,
These days, you know jobs are not easy to get
You'll jeopardise everything, and fall into debt!'

When finished, at the base, his name he signed
Stevie looked on, he was now quite resigned
That Johnny would lose his job, for sure,
No longer to work on the factory floor!

'Now, you take it to him, as soon as you arrive
I'm staying at home, I'm going to skive,'
Stevie agreed, it was all he could do
He'd already tried to air his view!

Johnny left Stevie, and laughed all the way
It was a nasty trick, on his mate, to play,
For the pen was of the joke shop kind
Blank paper is all the boss would find!

But when Johnny got home his mood soon changed
It was as though he was a man deranged
His trick had backfired, there was nothing more sure
As the invisible ink pen, he found, on the floor!

Rats!

Rats, rats, everywhere they are lined
In cages, stacked up, hundreds combined,
Why breed them, you ask, what purpose to serve?
The closer you get, the tougher your nerve!

The answer is easy, the breeder will tell
He keeps their cages clean, their doings to sell,
Bred for their by-product and nothing more
Which is used to make ratchet spanners galore!

High Panic!

The rustlers took to the air in spirits high
As they made their escape through the sky,
Six big cows and ten fat sheep
Stolen from the farmer's keep!

The animals were frightened, the rustlers were too
As panic set in, the plane tilted askew,
They had no choice, or they would crash
To open the door they made a dash.

Down below, a fishing boat was sailing by
The captain gave a nervous cry,
He woke his crew from carefree sleep
Shouting, 'Look, it's raining cows and sheep!'

Paul's Place

The pub was deserted as Paul took his seat
A stranger in town, facing defeat,
When a regular appeared and gave him a look
Asked him to move, his head he shook.

'You can't sit there, that's my place
Every night I'm here,' he pulled a face,
Paul objected, suggesting he sit elsewhere
He was there first, it just wasn't fair.

The agitated man then the publican did call
Insisting that he must evict poor Paul,
Still Paul wouldn't move, it was his right
Until told, '*You* then must play the piano tonight!'

Tamagotchi Mad!

A Tamagotchi's taken over in our house you could say
Cherished, loved and pampered throughout every night
and day,
A pet that cannot breathe, with no beating heart within
This small electronic being, mesmerising much-loved kin.

Half the household in favour of this Tamagotchi craze
The other quite demented at its most demanding ways,
No time for any other, an all-consuming passion
The Tamagotchi's presence making resentment quite the
fashion.

The situation could not go on, I wished it soon would die
This Tamagotchi seemed so much better loved than I,
For it to live much longer, I could not cope with that
So my mother's Tamagotchi, I drowned in cooking fat!

The Nice Man

The nice man, and his granny, stopped to buy a car
The salesman looked excited, as they eyed a Jaguar,
A test drive was requested, the salesman was in doubt
As the only one on duty, he could not take them out.

'No matter,' said the nice man, 'I'll leave my granny here
I'll take a spin around the block, never ever fear.'
This was the right solution, the salesman agreed
Of a healthy fat commission, he was readily in need!

So the nice man drove the car away, leaving far behind
The salesman and the lady, he promised he would mind,
A stranger from the old folks home, he'd picked up on the
    way
In a car he'd stolen earlier – it was his lucky day!

From Cradle to Grave

A slap at birth sets the course for life
Kicked through childhood, an early strife,
Rapped as a teenager, constantly misunderstood
All things bad, outweigh the good.

Cursed as an adult, nowhere to flee
Though the world is vast, you're never free,
Trapped in a society, harsh and cold
And worse it gets, as you grow old.

Sorrow and grief, all come your way
From cradle to grave, it's the price you pay,
Rumour has it that reborn one day we'll be
But once is enough, never again for me!

Opposites Attract

Vicki was smart but not very bright
Her life was dark, she needed light,
She must look forward and never look back
In abundance it was love she did lack.

Never on her own, she was often alone
Though disapproval she could not condone,
Her parents 'not understanding', though well they did
She sought someone special, a common bid.

Her mates she was close to, though far away
To pick herself up, she'd slip down for the day,
Take a bus, when she needed a lift
Though she had to pay, it was to prove a gift.

She went out to stay 'in' with her mates
Longingly wishing for no shortage of dates,
For her dreams to become a fact of real life
To gain a husband and become a wife.

When down in town, she called her mates up
Arranged a time and place to sup,
Their easy company was hard to beat
She'd win the game, not face defeat.

Showing no fear, bravado she felt
For the cards on the table were being dealt,
Stating her past would hold the future key
A chance meeting was her destiny!

Her future intended was a boy from her past
Last evening, their first, the die was cast,
To this end, she'd met him, and together they'd start
Happy together, never ever to part!

Farm Visit

On a visit to a farm in Crook
The geese got a quizzical look
'Do they bite?'
Asked Jimmy White
'No, but they'd give you a nasty suck!'

Peter's Pink Pyjamas

Peter wore a pair of pink pyjamas
Quite convinced, it would alarm us
But we honestly think
His colour is pink
With or without his pyjamas!

My Critic

I write a line, he doesn't rate it
He suggests another, sometimes I hate it!
Others, it's better, I have to agree
Then it's his line on the page you will see!

I think the words fit in quite well
But he sees it different he has to tell,
'This line is too long, that's too short
You'll have to give it far more thought!'

He says, 'The verse is in the wrong place,'
So to keep him happy, I change its base,
Then, 'This word is wrong and it should go,'
But which one to use, he doesn't know!

Sometimes I think I've confounded the chap,
When he finds no faults, I'm ready to clap,
But the very last line he says is wrong
Invariably, of course, 'It's far too long!'

But this critic of mine, I would not be without
For my poems are improved without a doubt,
And I wreak my revenge when his poems I see
For who's his critic? Of course, it's me!

It's Over!

'It's over,' he said – I was all forlorn
For ever together, he'd always sworn,
But now he'd discarded all that we had
The parting, for me, was immensely sad.

What went wrong, he never made clear
His love diminished, I sadly fear,
There was no one else, I heard him say
Before I turned from him and walked away!

To pick up the pieces I had to do
Get on with my life, find love anew,
The heartache was deep, he'd been my life
I'd hoped one day to be his wife!

Many weeks later, he was to reappear
He'd made a mistake, he made it clear,
He regretted his decision that tore us apart
And wanted, with me, to make a fresh start.

My heart leapt within a body that shook
As he gazed at me, with inquisitive look,
'It's over,' I said, 'never together, I've sworn,'
My love was diminished – he left forlorn!

One's Pig

A sty is for keeping one's pig in
Where it can, if it wants, make a big din
For it likes a sty
To comfortably lie
With bedding to root and dig in!

Chippendale Style

It was party time for the ladies this night
They were to cheer and squeal in delight,
As male strippers, in Chippendale style
Cavorted on stage, in single file.

Peggy, in her forties, was having the time of her life
Abandoning her sedate role as mother and wife
For just a night to shriek loud and long
At each of the strippers, to remove his thong!

Then Peggy's face changed, when she recognised her son
Peeling off his scant garments, until he was done,
Not since a child had she seen him undress
He'd grown somewhat she had to confess!

The Workmen

The workmen came one summer's day
I saw them arrive from my window bay
It was obvious they were preparing to stay
That their job would take more than just a day.

For two days they worked, not once did I pry
Though to guess their motive, I admit I did try,
But it was their business and none of mine
I kept a low profile, until up went a sign.

It was clear then, a bus shelter they'd erected,
I had to wonder whose instructions had directed
A bus shelter painstakingly and professionally done
In a street where buses have long ceased to run!

Waiting to Dine!

The restaurant was busy as we prepared to wait
The fourth couple, in line, for a dinner date
After thirty minutes, the first couple, in disgust
Left the restaurant as they quietly cussed!

Impatient they'd been, they'd go elsewhere
Somewhere with ample tables spare,
Then, when a name was called, and no one responded
We assumed it must be that of the couple absconded.

We nodded to the waitress, it was a first class chance
To jump the queue, our dinner to advance,
'At last you're here, please come on through
All your family, at the table, are waiting for you!'

Five Sisters

Five sisters were travelling on their regular route
One was big, the smallest was cute,
The three middle sisters were of average size
Always together at each fall and rise!

They were cramped, there was not much room
It was always dark, they travelled in gloom
Constantly on the move, throughout the long day
Keeping pace with each other, every step of the way.

Though well cared for, sometimes life was a toil
Incurring cuts and sores, their features to spoil
Life could be hard for five sisters; each a stunner,
Being the toes, on the foot, of a long distance runner!

Dustbin Day

Debbie was up early knowing Wednesday was dustbin day
As she collected her bin bags, on the pavement to lay,
She was the first on this sunny morn
To clear all her rubbish so soon after dawn.

She ate her breakfast before leaving for work
Her neighbours had been busy, she had to smirk,
For all along the street black bin bags were lined
Tied up neatly for the bin men to find.

Nothing unusual about this, you might say
Except Debbie had erred – it was only Tuesday
Which just goes to show that people will leap
To an instant conclusion and follow like sheep!

Noisy Neighbours

Of their next door neighbours, they'd had their fill
So they were moving away, it gave them a thrill,
No more noise, or disturbance to bear
No more would these people be constantly there.

The house they'd bought was in a decent neighbourhood
With everyone renowned for being quiet and good
At last they could settle and enjoy their life
Without noisy neighbours to cause them strife.

They'd found themselves the perfect place
Peaceful and quiet a friendly base,
Even when their nice neighbours decided to move
Still sure, of new neighbours, they would approve.

They could not believe it when they were to see
Who their new next door neighbours turned out to be,
For it was the old ones, by a stroke of bad luck
Noisy neighbours again, with whom they were stuck!

Tranquil Water

She knelt to pray at the water side
A tranquil place, her guilt to hide,
Her mind was confused, tormented too
As she cast her eyes on waters blue.

The tranquillity, no reflection of her inner pain
A precious love lost, her turmoil was plain,
Beside the still water, contemplating her sin
Kneeling in prayer, seeking forgiveness within.

The water gently lapped the shore
She would find no peace at heaven's door,
Her faithless love, she cast out to drown
In this tranquil water, weighted down!

Carpet Capers

Jan was browsing the shops while waiting for a lift
When she spotted a carpet, a positive gift,
A remnant piece, though not that small
Which would fit quite nicely in the hall.

She bought the carpet there and then
Assisted to the car park by two nice men,
She waited a few minutes for her husband to appear
Thankful the weather was warm, sunny and clear.

Bob would soon pick her up in his transit van
He was never late, a most punctual man,
His arrival then made her gasp and stare
As he stopped on his motorbike beside her there!

Bob looked at the carpet then he looked Jan's way,
'Well,' he explained, 'it was such a nice day
I thought today I'd leave the van behind
That you could ride pillion, you wouldn't mind!'

'Now, I can see it's not a possible choice,'
He fought to control his breaking voice
He doubled with laughter and helplessly fell,
'You can't ride pillion with a carpet as well!'

Dentist Bill

There was a dentist called Bill
Who derived pleasure when using his drill
His patients all hated
The way it vibrated
Only Bill, with his drill, got a thrill!

Policeman Paul

There was a policeman called Paul
Who was six feet and six inches tall
Though he looked up in respect
He looked down to detect
His superior was awfully small!

Mabel's Hat

Mabel's hat was an abominable apparel
Given to her by sweet cousin Daryl,
But it was ugly, she had to admit
She would not enjoy wearing it one little bit.

She put it away, well out of sight
Not wishing her friends to take delight
In the fact that dear sweet cousin Daryl
Had no taste at all when choosing apparel!

But his feelings she would never hurt
That she hated the hat she wouldn't alert,
For his intentions were most remarkably good
She'd wear it for him, she knew she would.

When next she saw him, she wore the hat
The first time ever, you can be sure of that!
He met her with a smile and wondrous eyes
As he looked at the hat in total surprise!

'Your charity shop was to benefit from that
How could you wear such an ugly hat?'
He stared in wonder at Mabel's apparel
He too hated the hat – sweet cousin Daryl!

Master of my Mind!

I didn't do it, it wasn't me
Who wrote this book, can't you see?
The talent people think is mine
Comes deep within, a power divine!

Control of it I do not possess
My credibility is hard to assess,
How is it done? Who puts them there?
The words, the sentiment, the poetic flair?

Who is the master of my mind
Taking it over, as words are consigned
To paper, where they flow with ease,
Someone tell me, who is he, please?

While he exists, I'll take the glory
Though here I tell the real story
When he visits, I'm assured of success
The talent is his, not mine to possess!

As long as he stays, it's easy for me
To feign my talent, for all to see
But, I fear, some day I'll find
He's left, this master of my mind!